D1105089

Tasso and Milton

Tasso and Milton

The Problem of Christian Epic

Judith A. Kates

Lewisburg
Bucknell University Press
London and Toronto: Associated University Presses

© 1983 by Associated University Presses, Inc.

Associated University Presses, Inc.
440 Forsgate Drive
Cranbury, NJ 08512

Associated University Presses Ltd
25 Sicilian Avenue
London WC1A 2QH, England

Associated University Presses
2133 Royal Windsor Drive
Unit 1
Mississauga, Ontario, Canada L5J 1K5

Library of Congress Cataloging in Publication Data

Kates, Judith A., 1941–
    Tasso and Milton, the problem of Christian epic.

    Bibliography: p.
    Includes index.
    1. Tasso, Torquato, 1544–1595.   Gerusalemme
liberata.   2. Milton, John, 1608–1674.   Paradise
lost.   3. Christianity in literature.   4. Godfrey,
of Bouillon, ca. 1060–1100—Poetry.   5. Crusades—
First, 1096–1099—Poetry.   I. Title.
PQ4656.K37   1983   809.1'3   82-71268
ISBN 0-8387-5046-X

Printed in the United States of America

For Bill

Contents

Preface

During his Italian journey of 1638–39, John Milton enjoyed the attentions of a Neapolitan nobleman, Giovanni Battista Manso. If we are to judge from the dedication to the Latin poem Milton composed for him as a gesture of gratitude, his most distinctive claims to praise derived from his friendship with Torquato Tasso.[1] The figure of Tasso appears repeatedly in the poem, a compelling image of the "magnus poeta," the great poet, whom the young Englishman longs to resemble, as he tells us through the elaborate classical allusions of the poem's hundred lines. Why Tasso? How could this poet of romantic longing and operatic melancholy figure for Milton as the Italian Virgil, his poem the great example of contemporary epic?

I propose, in this book, to make sense of Tasso's continuing presence for Milton, when he came at last to his enterprise "of highest hope and hardest attempting,"[2] *Paradise Lost*. For Tasso, like Milton after him, accomplished that feat toward which Renaissance poets continually struggled, the re-creation of classical epic in a form and language congruent with Christian vision. Tasso, in full awareness, grappled with the "problem" of Christian epic— the need to create a recognizably epic narrative, while transforming such heroic poetry into a vehicle for the exploration of the inner life, the truly significant life for a Christian. *La Gerusalemme liberata*, in my reading, shifts the arena of epic heroism inward, toward the moral and psychological, and yet preserves an allegiance to classical form. I account for that development partially by setting the poem in the context of contemporary thought about the nature of heroic poetry, emphasizing particularly Tasso's eclectic description of the ideal epic.

9

This account also suggests that the critical context in which Tasso worked was not an obstacle course, barely survived, but the foundation for some of the more fruitful literary and moral issues confronted in the poem.

Both Tasso and Milton were enormously learned poets who heroically transcended erudition. Like almost everyone at the time, they saw the writing of epic as the supreme enterprise for a poet. Tasso began essays in heroic poetry at the age of eighteen. Milton prepared himself for years for his "great Argument." *La Gerusalemme liberata* and *Paradise Lost* both reflect self-conscious consideration of vast reading in ancient and contemporary works, as any cursory glance at studies of their "sources" or notes to the poems will reveal.

But they also were written at moments which the clarity of hindsight now reveals to have been crucial in the radical alteration of consciousness that we call "modern" and perceive as beginning in the Renaissance. In Italy in the sixteenth century and England in the seventeenth century, the shifting balance of what, for the sake of simplicity, we call secular and religious concerns made a synthesizing coherence of view more and more difficult to achieve. The writing of epic, dependent as it was on an inclusive vision, reveals most dramatically the conflicting allegiances and consequent strains in intellectual and moral life. The very idea of a Christian epic incorporates such strains. "Epic," by definition, implied the pagan cultures of Greece and Rome and the humanist response to those cultures. It also assumed an enlargement of the human, an intense energizing of the life of this mortal earth. "Christian" implied an opposing perception and response to experience more preoccupied with the paradox of life after death, and ways of bringing mortal life into conformity with it. Christian values and ideals changed the way people read epic poetry and what they expected of it.[3] But the need to weld together opposing values, ideas, literary qualities remained a condition of writing in the genre. In many ways, the writing of both these poems embodied a heroic enterprise in itself. They triumph over conflict, and emerge whole precisely when the malaise of divided consciousness became inescapably apparent in postmedieval Europe. They achieve an inclusive and coherent vision when it had begun to seem impossible. In their respective languages, they represent the last such achievements. In Italian after Tasso and in English after Milton, serious epic on the grand scale is never successfully written again.

In exploring my perception that Tasso and Milton constructed their poems out of a similarly problematic relationship to epic tradition, I devote the lion's share of my discussion to Tasso, whose work has received much less attention along these lines. I proceed, therefore, from an analysis of his theoretical writing on epic poetry in the context of sixteenth-century Italian criticism and theory to a detailed reading of *La Gerusalemme liberata* as a whole. My final chapter, suggesting analogies with *Paradise Lost*, assumes greater familiarity with Milton's text and critical commentary on it.

All translations from Tasso's poetry and prose are my own. Other translations from Italian are mine, unless otherwise noted.

Acknowledgments

Quotations from *The Faerie Queene* are from *The Poetical Works of Edmund Spenser* edited by J. C. Smith and E. de Selincourt, 1912 (repr. 1961) and are reprinted by permission of Oxford University Press. Parts of chapters 3 and 6 appeared in different form in my article, "The Revaluation of the Classical Heroic in Tasso and Milton," published in *Comparative Literature*, Fall, 1974, and are reprinted by kind permission of the editor.

I acknowledge with gratitude the aid and encouragement I received at various stages in the preparation of this book from Dante Della Terza, Walter J. Kaiser, Harry Levin, the late Reuben A. Brower, the late Isabel G. MacCaffrey, Morton W. Bloomfield, Adele M. Dalsimer, Patricia M. Spacks, Rachel Jacoff and Dorrit Cohn. I benefited greatly from a fellowship year at the Bunting (formerly Radcliffe) Institute for Independent Study. I owe special thanks to Margery M. Sabin. My sons, Robert B. Kates and Thomas J. Kates, sustained me with their confidence and good cheer. My dedication can only suggest my thankfulness for the unfailing support of my husband, William W. Kates.

Tasso and Milton

1

The Critical Context

IN the flood of literary energy of the sixteenth and seventeenth centuries in Europe, we can distinguish a special group of writers, the creators of both poetry and literary theory. Tasso, like Ronsard, Sidney, or Dryden, occupies an outstanding place in this group. His epic on the first crusade, *La Gerusalemme liberata*, was preceded, accompanied, and followed by a profuse outpouring of critical and theoretical writing from the poet himself. The enormous tangle of contemporary disputes posed problems which he had to resolve before poetic creation could proceed satisfactorily. He formulated solutions for such vexed issues as unity and variety, verisimilitude and the marvelous, epic and romance. In so doing, he placed demands on his own poem which contributed to the dramatic conflicts that form much of its power.

Many of the crucial critical debates in the Italian sixteenth century arose from attempts to evaluate the special excellences of the classical epics or to define the ideal epic, the genre accepted by most thinkers as the noblest and most valuable. Tasso contributed to this continuing discussion in his early *Discorsi*, the *Lettere poetiche*, and even in the preface to his youthful epic, *Rinaldo*. With the appearance of the *Gerusalemme liberata*, the analysis of his own masterpiece incited major public arguments. The significance of such theoretical formulations for Tasso went far beyond technical considerations. Fundamental moral and intellectual convictions were implied in his interpretation of Aristotle, his choice of the *Poetics* as the important authority on the nature of art, his insistence that epic and romance constitute one genre, and in his choice

17

of a historical subject. A half-century of debate produced a fairly
clear sense of the moral and literary values associated with traditional forms and uses of language. The *Discorsi* reveal Tasso's
sophisticated perception of the larger meanings implicit in technical choices of form or subject matter, and the consequent posi-
tioning of a piece of literature within a particular tradition. The
conception of epic that he develops in the early *Discorsi* makes
inevitable the choice of subject in the *Gerusalemme*. That conception also explains his effort to expand the epic genre to include,
rather than oppose, many of the attributes of Italian romance. The
tensions created by the necessity to weld a coherent whole out of
the "varietà" of characters and episodes are resolved in a new sense
of what constitutes heroic poetry.

When we examine the critical background out of which Tasso's
theory and practice grew, we discover the moral, even spiritual
value, associated with the "rules"—the abstract conception of the
form and the principles that must govern its composition. The
need for coherence, for genuine unity welded out of variety, is felt
by the poet as a moral need. Theoretical ideas on what makes a
poem good are also statements of values. The good poem is aesthetically right and a moral act on the side of right reason, of
spiritual goodness.

Most of Tasso's ideas about heroic poetry, taken point by point,
were not original or new, though they are particularly well expressed.[1] Like most of his contemporaries, he derived his ideas
from a fusion of Horace and Aristotle, fostered by a plethora of
sixteenth-century commentaries on both classical authors and by
original "arts of poetry" from such older writers as Trissino or
Minturno.[2] But Tasso's work is striking in its sound eclecticism.
He was able to mediate effectively between the emerging polarities
in critical thought—between the champions of Ariosto's romantic
narrative and the defenders of a strict classicism, the "moderns"
and the "ancients." His compromises allowed him to include what
looked like opposites at the time, and therefore to preserve all
aspects of the epic tradition as it had been revealed by his predecessors' discussion and practice of it.

A central assumption with pervasive influence on Tasso's theory
and practice was the Christian interpretation of Horace's advice to
blend pleasure and utility.[3]

Omne tulit punctum qui miscuit utile dulci,
lectorem delectando pariterque monendo.

(*Ars Poetica*, ll. 343–44)

(He has won every vote who has blended profit and pleasure, at once delighting and instructing the reader)

Horace mentions these literary goals with egalitarian symmetry:

> Aut prodesse volunt aut delectare poetae
> aut simul et iucunda et idonea dicere vitae.
>
> (Ll. 333–34)

(Poets aim either to benefit or to amuse, or to utter words at once both pleasing and helpful to life)

Though meant seriously, the advice to combine *utilis* and *dulcis* is proffered in a semihumorous vein, not only with the image of winning votes, but in the promise that this is the key to money for the booksellers and fame for the author.[4]

> hic meret aera liber Sosiis, hic et mare transit
> et longum noto scriptori prorogat aevum.
>
> (Ll. 345–46)

(That is the book to make money for the Sosii; this the one to cross the sea and extend to a distant date its author's fame)

Almost all sixteenth century writers took this as an authoritative dictum. But the idea that poetry must combine pleasure and profit received varying emphases. Vida, in his elaborate manual on the ideal epic (1527), echoes Horace's advice by urging the poet to add memorable moral *sententiae* to the delights of variety.

> With gay descriptions sprinkle here and there
> Some grave instructive sentences with care,
> That touch on life, some moral good pursue,
> . . . .
> Rules which the future sire may make his own,
> And point the golden precepts to his son.[5]

Giraldi Cintio, Tasso's antagonist in the epic-romance controversy, begins his discussion of romances (1554) by considering the poet's choice of material. The notion that his goal is the dual one of pleasure and utility is so firmly embedded that it appears almost parenthetically. "The material which the talented man uses and the art with which he writes being, then, of greatest importance, he ought to exercise the utmost care in choosing the material with which a writer may work laudably, such as has the potential for ornament and splendor, such as can be pleasing and useful [*grata ed utile*] to one who will devote himself to reading his composition." But when Cintio states the poet's goal explicitly, his interpretation of the Horatian statement receives the emphasis common to most Christian thinkers. "In the composition of Romances the fable should be founded upon one or more illustrious actions, which the poet may imitate suitably with pleasant language, to teach men honest life and good customs, which should be the foremost end of composing for any good poet."[6]

This assumption of the primacy of moral goals characterized sixteenth-century thinkers, heirs of a long Christian-Platonic tradition. So pervasive and congenial was the idea that the text of Aristotle's *Poetics*, little known until the sixteenth century, often was interpreted as expressing the same view. Thus Cintio: "Aristotle said that the poet's aim was to induce good mores in the minds of men; . . . whereas the historian ought to write only the facts and actions as they are, the poet shows not things as they are but as they ought to be for the ameliorizing of life" (p. 51). Bernardo Tasso, Torquato's father, insists upon poetry's moral function in the context of a defense against Plato's banishment of poets in the *Republic* (1562). The poet's function, he says, is "by imitating human actions through the delightfulness of plots, through the sweetness of the words arranged in a most beautiful order, through the harmony of the verse, to adorn human souls with good and gentle characters, and with various virtues."[7] Aesthetic pleasures provide the means through which poets can achieve moral ends. In the second version of his *Discorsi* (1594), written late in life, Torquato Tasso assesses the two Horatian goals quite similarly. He actually quotes the relevant line from *Ars Poetica* ("Aut prodesse volunt aut delectare poetae") in his opening pages. But he argues that poetry really has only one goal, for the best poetry is directed toward benefit or profit (*il giovamento*).[8] He defines poetry as "the imitation of human actions so as to benefit through pleasing [*affine di giovar dilettando*]" (p. 69). The statement, reflecting both Aristotle and Horace, demotes pleasure from the equal grammatical status accorded it in the Horatian phrasing. Through this syntax, moral utility as the crucial verb dominates merely adjectival delight.

Christian insistence on the fallen state of humanity lies behind such a hierarchical ordering of the aesthetic and moral effects of literature. Because fallen man prefers pleasure to righteousness, he can be led to respond to the ideas necessary for salvation more easily through the delights of beautiful language and engaging stories. Therefore, the excellence of a work depends on its capacity to give precepts for the good life pleasurably. This evaluation of imaginative literature especially suited sixteenth-century Italian thinking in general. An obsessive search for moral seriousness and religious justification distinguished this from earlier humanist culture in Italy. The religiosity that characterized the "new learning" in northern Europe from the beginning, developed with the convert's zeal in this period of Italian culture. In the positions taken by critics and theorists, it is certainly possible to demonstrate an analogy to the general stance given Italian intellectual life by the Council of Trent. Poetry, though by definition created to give pleasure, was justified by insisting on the purely instrumental value of its special delights.

For this purpose, writers continually fell back on the old image of the "sweet medicine." Tasso calls aesthetic pleasure the "honey anointing the cup when medicine is given to children," if it serves moral ends. If it is an end in itself, it has "the effect of a deadly poison" and "keeps minds occupied in vain reading" (p. 67). His father, too, had alluded to this image in the overtly Platonic context of his defense of poetry. Plato, he said, had not meant to exclude all poets. He would have banished only those who "aroused and inflamed the tender souls of young people to lascivious and voluptuous actions . . ." and were therefore "like a wicked doctor who gives poison instead of medicine."[9] The image, derived ultimately from Plato himself,[10] appears in Tasso's late *Discorsi* to express the more narrowly moral orientation he developed toward poetry in the final years of his life. Readers are like children who must be deceived by a sweet surface into imbibing the moral nourishment hidden underneath. Like his father, he distinguished the best poets who consciously use the aesthetic and emotional pleasures of literature for moral ends from those who care only about pleasing their readers. Tasso's language here echoes his version of the image in the *Gerusalemme liberata* (*Discorsi*, p. 67, "quel mele di cui s'unge il vaso quando si dà la medicina a'fanciulli," that honey with which one smears the cup when one gives medicine to children; *Gerusalemme liberata* I, 3, "Così a l'egro fanciul porgiamo aspersi/ Di soavi licor gli orli del vaso," so to the sick child we offer the edges of the cup sprinkled with sweet syrups).[11] But in the poem it serves as an introduction to a complicated and subtle revaluation of the classical culture from which Tasso derived his aesthetic norms (see chapter 3).

This Christian-Platonic ordering of moral and aesthetic elements in imaginative literature was not always Tasso's response to the traditional Horatian version of the ends of poetry. Indeed, in some of his early critical statements, such as the youthful lecture, *Lezione sopra un sonetto di Monsignor Della Casa*, of about 1565, he states quite plainly that he believes the end of poetry is *delectare*: ". . . since the poet must delight, either because pleasure is his end, as I believe, or because it is a necessary means to bring about utility, as others judge, he is not a good poet who does not delight. . . ."[12]

The earlier version of the *Discorsi*, produced just before the poem itself,[13] creates a stable equilibrium between *prodesse* and *delectare*. It assumes the ultimate moral aim of literature. The idealization of human characters and actions, the concern for the validity and power conferred by truth or seeming-truth, and other aspects of the whole problem of effects on the audience (all of this to be discussed in more detail later) reflect the assumption of a moral purpose. But this is not the operational basis of his theory. In practice, the *Discorsi* imply, the poet operates as though he aims for aesthetic pleasure. As poet, he works only toward this goal, though as citizen, he seeks to give pleasure as the most effective means of teaching. ". . . the poet must pay a great deal of attention to profit, if not because he is a poet (for that is not his goal [*fine*] as poet) at least because he is a citizen [*uomo civile*] and part of the state [*republica*]" (p. 9). As a result of this balancing of the two aims of poetry, he incorporates traditional moral assumptions into an aesthetically oriented personal theory, based on the *Poetics* of Aristotle.

Tasso was creating his own theoretical structure for epic poetry at a time when the text of the *Poetics* had already been much debated. Many commentators had clarified the varieties of implications that could be drawn from Aristotle's work. Older writers whose work was important to Tasso, like Minturno, Speroni, and Scaliger had already worked at literary problems using Aristotelian terms and criteria for judgment. Since Aristotle's discussion of epic was relatively brief, the critics took on the major task of creating a poetics for this form. They strove to use what they interpreted as Aristotelian concepts to define the ideal epic.

For Tasso, Aristotle was of central importance in the analysis of the aesthetic principles for shaping a heroic poem. Like the *Poetics*, the *Discorsi dell'arte poetica* differentiate elements that are important to the poem as an entity in itself. In his concern about unity, coherence, proportion, and completeness, Tasso concentrates on factors that one considers in looking at the poem aesthetically.

And yet Tasso's Aristotelianism does not represent a completely "aesthetic" mode of criticism contrasting with the "moral" poetics of others. On the contrary, Aristotelianism comes to imply a whole moral vision that is essential to the definition and judgment of the epic in his theory and to the quality of the poem itself. In the first place, the prevailing attitudes of cultured and scholarly men supported a criticism based on Aristotelian principles. Scaliger, in 1561, declared Aristotle to be the perpetual dictator of all the arts. More generally, skill and erudition in the Greek philosopher's writings signified a genuinely impressive cultivation, whose products could be taken seriously as a matter of course. To modern critics this has looked like cultural oppression, operating to redirect energies that would have found more congenial expression in other philosophical tendencies.[14]

But Tasso constructs a more positive relationship with Aristotelian theory. Not only does it allow him to create a practical criticism that judges poetry on its own terms, but it connects aesthetic precepts to philosophical truths. He sees Aristotelian principles as expressions of natural reason, that faculty of the human mind which operates in harmony with the natural laws that govern all of creation. Because art is an imitation of nature, there is a "nature of things" in art as eternal and immutable as in nature itself. What is judged to be beautiful by applying natural reason must always be beautiful, because neither nature nor reason can change in any essential way. Aristotle deals with the nature of poetic things, and therefore he is still the greatest source of wisdom on the art. His position, based as it is on deductions of natural reason, reflects nature. This makes him not so much an authority on poetry, as the voice of the unchanging truths of the art.

Tasso argues this out explicitly and in considerable detail in the course of the quarrel with the pro-Arioso critics in the years after the publication of his *Gerusalemme*. In 1585, he published a defense of the *Poetics* as a reply to an attack on Aristotle by Francesco Patrizi *(Discorso sopra il parere fatto del sig. Francesco Patricio, in difesa di Ludovico Ariosto.)*.[15] Patrizi had designed his treatise to dismiss the rules which had been used, during the controversy, to attack the *Orlando furioso*. He had established a general anti-Aristotelian position, declaring that Aristotle's teachings are not proper or true, do not form a scientific art of poetry, should not be used to judge poetry, and were not derived from the practice of ancient poets. Tasso affirms the opposite. He considers these principles "proper" because they have to do only with poetry, and with no other art or form of discourse, and because they are the first principles by *nature*. He considers Aristotle's principles true because they deal with truth and verisimilitude. And they are sufficient, because no others are needed to define and describe the whole nature of the art. The foundation of the *Poetics* in natural reason, rather than in experience, custom, or usage, all of which are admittedly transient and debatable, removes Aristotle's discussion from the realm of arguable opinion to that of fact.

In this polemically motivated discourse, we can see explicitly argued out the assumption that directs much of the early *Discorsi*, a more private document as it deals with issues that became important in the actual production of his own epic. Aristotelian ideas and arguments based on them are convincing and finally authoritative because they result from the operation of natural reason, and are of necessity in harmony with Nature itself. When Aristotle analyzed the components of a beautiful poem, he articulated the structure of Beauty. Through deduction from Aristotle's principles, we can reveal the foundations for a poem true to nature and valid because it emerges from man's highest faculty, his reason. This evaluation of the *Poetics* speaks to the old debate about the importance of learned, rationally constructed art vs. divinely granted, inexplicable inspiration. Tasso, while granting the ultimate necessity of an inspired quality for literary greatness, really embraces, as a practicing poet, truths about the poetic art discovered through the exercise of reason.

This in itself implies a moral judgment on poetry as a human activity. It directs the evaluation of poetry toward one side of the continuing debate about the place of imaginative literature in the moral scheme of things. If poetry is produced according to principles discovered in nature by reason, then it is, by nature, an activity of a high moral order. It expresses truth in matter, and its manner accords with the natural and moral laws governing all human behavior. Properly functioning reason could deduce only such principles. And man's reason, even in the fallen world, does operate in harmony with the nature of things as God created it and discovers truth, when not perverted by sin. Given the assumption of Tasso's culture that Aristotle's mind operated without fault, his reasoning on the nature of poetry carries moral as well as dialectic weight. Because Tasso, and Renaissance thinkers in general, believed in correspondence between human reason and objective truth about the divinely ordered world, to reason truly meant to perceive the good. In that context, a poetics based on Aristotle becomes in itself a moral declaration about the purpose and proper creation of poetic art.

Tasso assumes such an evaluation of the classical foundation for his ideas in the *Discorsi*. It emerges most pervasively and impressively in the dominant strain of imagery in the work through which he creates analogies between the organization and structure of poetic genres and the ordering of all living things in the natural world. In the most constant strain of natural imagery in the *Discorsi*, he talks repeatedly of "genus" and "species." For instance, in his all-important discussion of whether or not epic and romance actually constitute different genres:

> If the romance is a species to be distinguished from epic, it is clear that they are distinguished by some essential difference; accidental differences cannot create a difference in species. But since one cannot find any specific difference between romance and epic, it clearly follows that there is no distinction in species to be found between them. (P. 26)

Aside from the importance of the position defended here, to which I shall return, the striking feature of the passage is the ease with which Tasso falls into the metaphor. It requires no explanation, no "as if" or "like." Such facility with the metaphor of natural order is based on the fact that art is defined from the first as in Aristotle, an imitation of nature.

One can find any number of such general assertions of the analogy between "artificial" and natural forms used as the basis for defending a specific position on literary questions. For example, in relation to the idea of unity of action, Tasso bases an argument essential to his whole concept of the epic on such an analogy:

> As in every other poem, those poems which deal with the deeds [*armi*] and loves of heroes and knights-errant and which are called by the general [*comune*] name, heroic poems, must be one [*una*] in plot [*favola*] and form. But we call a form "one" in several ways. We call one the form of the elements, which is very simple, with simple powers [*virtù*] and simple effect [*operazione*]. We also call one the form of plants and animals: but this form is mixed and is the composite result of the elemental structures brought together, blunted and altered, partaking of the qualities and effects of each single element. So likewise in poetry we find some simple and some composite forms. . . . (P. 37)

Aside from the general expression of the "natural" metaphor here, there is again an assumed, unargued conception which that metaphor asserts. And it is all the more convincing as an aesthetic position, because Tasso handles it so easily as a stylistic technique, rather than as a philosophical argument. The aesthetic principles derived from reason (here, the principle of unity of action defined in a particular way) reflect the laws governing natural forms. In this passage the ordering of statements conveys that idea. Though he opens with his literary point, the next statements do not discuss the point in literary terms, with the natural analogy brought in as an explicit comparison. Rather, the discussion of unity of form as it is found in nature follows immediately, as though he were actually pursuing the topic in the same terms and not making use of an analogy at all. Tasso brings to bear all the authority and conviction of the argument from nature without actually acknowledging his use of an argument by analogy. As a result, when we do actually come to "so likewise in poetry," we almost lose the fact that a comparison has been made in the greater weight and complexity of the analysis of form in nature. Tasso can support his literary argument with all the conviction of ideas about nature manifestly true. At the same time he expresses, by the complete merging of the natural and literary terminology (e.g., "form") and by the ordering of his statements, the sense that the truths about the order of nature apply equally to the order of literature, that product of the human mind.

The forms of nature exist as defined abstract entities, whose characteristics any specific example will embody (e.g., the form of *elements,* the form of *plants*). "So likewise," the forms of poetry should, if rightly ordered, seek to embody that ideal form deduced by reason. Tasso is elsewhere quite explicit about this idea.

> Natural forms seek to achieve a determinate size, and are restricted within certain limits of largeness and smallness. They are not permitted by nature to go beyond or to fail to attain those limits. Similarly, artificial forms seek to achieve a determinate size. (P. 21)

These general statements do not occur in the abstract context of a philosophical discussion, but are brought in pragmatically, as the literary point calls them to mind. They reflect the author's assumptions and general philosophic orientations, which manifest themselves naturally in the course of his thinking on essential literary problems. The Platonic tone of the two preceding passages does not imply a totally coherent Platonism, but stems from a fairly generalized Renaissance view of the order of nature and of man's place in it. The ease and conviction of the argument by analogy to nature expresses that sense of the essential harmony between the human mind and the world in which it operates, and which it reflects. Similarly, the perception of the true relations between ideal forms and their specific embodiments depends on the basic congruity between the rightly ordered mind and the nature of things. Thus, to use a poetic form properly—to know its laws and embody them well in a specific poem—becomes a rational and therefore moral act. It means assenting to, and operating within, the true, morally right order of action and thought.

The question of the true form of an epic poem then becomes infinitely more pressing, from a moral point of view, than whether or not one approves of Aristotle. And it is based on philosophical premises more fundamental than ideas about effects on the audience. Questions of audience response do enter the picture because to talk about the poem's effect on the audience always, in the Renaissance, included the *moral* effect on the audience. Critics therefore argued about whether Aristotelian literary principles made a piece of literature more or less effective as moral instruction. But once it has been accepted that Aristotle represents the voice of truly operating reason, Aristotelian principles embody a moral position in themselves, even though they represent a more strictly literary approach to the judgment and evaluation of poetry.

The immediate corollary of this powerful connection between Aristotelian aesthetics and the order of nature is that those literary principles are as immutable as the laws of nature themselves. If art is founded on principles derived from the nature of things, by right reason, the basic rules of poetry are eternal, like nature and reason. The *Discorsi* are perfectly explicit on this point.

> But those things that are directly based on nature, and are good and praiseworthy in themselves, have nothing to do with convention [*consuetudine*] nor does the tyranny of custom [*uso*] hold sway over them. One of those things is unity of plot which by its very nature creates goodness and perfection in a poem. This has been true in every past age and will be true in every future age. Another of those things is appropriate behavior [*i costumi*]; not the behavior we refer to when we use the term customs [*usanze*], but that which has its roots fixed in nature. In the proper behavior of the boy, the old man, the rich man, the ruler, the poor man, and the man of lower class, what is appropriate in one age is appropriate in every age. If this were not the case,

Aristotle would not have spoken of such things, because he only spoke of those things which belong in the category of Art. Since Art is constant and determinate, it would be impossible to include in the rules of Art anything that is changeable or uncertain through its dependence on the instability of custom. Likewise, he would not have discussed unity of plot, if he had not judged it to be a necessary aspect of the work of art in every age. Those who want to base a new art on new custom destroy the nature of Art and reveal a misunderstanding of the nature of custom. (P. 33)

This passage clearly defends an "ancient" position in the late Renaissance quarrel of ancients vs. moderns. But Tasso's allegiance to the cause of the ancients does not stem from a naïve reverence for classical ideas, simply because they are classical. He is too sophisticated a reader to insist flatly on the indisputable authority of ancient writers, in the manner of a Vida or of earlier humanists. Rather, he enters the camp of the ancients because he believes Aristotle's ideas to be founded on eternal principles, to which all rational men of any time must assent. The ancient position bears all the moral weight of "those things that are directly based on nature, and are good and praiseworthy in themselves." In this way, Tasso can argue for the power and validity of classical precedent as much in terms of moral as of aesthetic rightness. He can support his specific literary ideas not only with the sanction of a classical authority which commands respect because of prevailing cultural attitudes, but also with the sanction of values more fundamental and pressing to his readers than any purely literary ideas. This, of course, makes the moral evaluation of classical models more complex than it is for those whose moral judgment depends on the mere presence or absence of the Christian religion in a work. Tasso never totally condemned pagan literature, because of this sense of the moral rightness expressed in the order and beauty of the classics.

The expression of this ancient position emerges most clearly and fruitfully in those parts of the *Discorsi* related to the great epic-romance controversy that extended over a good half of the century. It is worthwhile to investigate some of the issues as they were raised in that debate, because Tasso's treatment of them demonstrates beautifully how inclusive he was able to be, while establishing a distinctive, coherent position. Moreover, that inclusiveness is reflected in the poem, and there exploited to create much of the dramatic tension and greatness of the *Gerusalemme*.

The opposition to Tasso's ideas, the "modern" camp, was represented most significantly by Giraldi Cintio and also by Giovanni Battista Pigna (*I romanzi,* 1554).[16] These two published in a spirit of controversy, disputing over who originated the ideas in question. But despite the differences in their theories, they both were seen as modern champions, to be distinguished from ancients like Minturno and Tasso. The basic premise of this side in the controversy was the distinction between epic and romance. In answer to derogatory criticisms of romances, and particularly of Ariosto, in such places as Trissino's preface to his strictly classical epic, *L'Italia liberata dai goti,* Cintio defended the romance first and foremost by differentiating two types of heroic poem. He insisted that Aristotle's precepts, especially the principle of unity of action, which had been used against the vernacular romances, apply only to one sort of heroic poem—the epic. The epic is exemplified by the narrative poetry of Homer and Virgil, and quite properly conforms to rules and prescriptions derived from Aristotle and Horace. Romance, on the other hand, is a completely different genre, a type of heroic poem to which Aristotle's laws do not apply. Those laws relate only to poems of a "single action," and romance does not belong in that category. From Tasso's viewpoint Cintio dealt with the main objection to romances as they were developed in Italian tradition in a way that could only be called begging the question. Ariosto and other romance writers were derogated for not following the principle of unity of action. Cintio simply defined the romance as a heroic poem which does not limit itself to a single action.

Cintio proceeded to defend himself however, with a whole series of arguments that involve substantial differences from Tasso in their assumptions about poetry. He founded his "modern" argument on the premise that poetic forms vary with the passage of time. Therefore, poetic genres develop within a particular moment in cultural history, and are appropriate to that time. But historical change renders once-valid poetic genres inappropriate to a new age. So, in a letter defending Ariosto written to Giovanni Battista Pigna and published in 1554,[17] Cintio asserts that romance is a genre appropriate to the Italian linguistic and therefore poetic tradition. To support this he argues that both Italian and the romance genre are derived from the French, Spanish, and Provencal languages and cultures. Epic, on the other hand, belonged to Latin (and to Virgil), since Latin was derived from Greek, and therefore took over the appropriate literary genre. He also proclaims the general principle that writers should practice those genres appropriate to their times, and by which their contemporaries will be pleased. Therefore, an Italian living in the sixteenth century should write romance.

To promote romance as *the* Italian genre meant to create a poetics of the genre deliberately opposite to Aristotle's insistence on unity of action. Cintio prescribed for a truly contemporary narrative poem multiplicity of action and the addition of ornaments or "fillers" *(riempimenti),* in order to create episodes that will give variety and therefore more pleasure. And he insisted that the poet should interrupt the flow of action to obtain suspense and prevent satiety, using digressions, and disturbances of the natural plot order. In other words, the narrative of some hypothetical great Italian poem should be constructed just like the *Orlando furioso.*

Cintio also supported his position by arguing from the traditional moral view of poetry. Like many Renaissance defenders of poetry, he argued from the premise that imaginative literature is valuable because it creates an idealized version of reality. He transforms into an ethical requirement Aristotle's distinction between the poet and the historian (the poet relates events that *could* happen, while the historian relates what *did* happen). The poet must present what should be. The important and ultimate aim of poetry, "moral improvement," is to be achieved by a poetry in which characters and plot are ordered and defined as moral precepts would have them. Cintio claimed that romance fulfills these aims much more completely and effectively than epic. He supported this view by arguing that romance is a genre developed from a Christian rather than pagan tradition. It is naturally adapted to the decorum of the Christian religion, a decorum necessary to the achievement of moral ends. He also contended that romance, whose techniques and structure arise from recent cultural developments, can more easily attract a contemporary audience, and therefore teach effectively. In this way, Cintio incorporated the basic Horatian principles into his polemic in favor of romance, and attempted to associate the moral weight of that line of argument with the "modern" side.

Though Tasso seems to have distorted Cintio's arguments to some extent, Cintio can reasonably be considered Tasso's antagonist in the controversy. Cintio's arguments present the main principles with which Tasso took issue in his own critical thinking. (More personally, there is the suggestion that Tasso's father decided to write a romance rather than a single-action epic like Trissino as a result of reading Cintio.) Cintio's defense of the romance form voiced ideas which Tasso found it necessary to oppose or, typically, to include in a qualified way in his own formulation of proper poetic practice in the narrative form. Although there were other arguments and other writers on the "modern" side with which Tasso was undoubtedly familiar, Cintio seems to offer the clearest and certainly the most characteristic expression of the assumptions and principles inherent in the "modern" position, as it relates to the debate over epic and romance.

Cintio's arguments were directly answered by a number of other critics, such as Speroni and Minturno,[18] the latter offering a major parallel to Tasso's thinking on this subject. As a result, the issues involved in the choice of form for the long narrative poem were being argued in a fairly extensive way when Tasso was beginning his major work.

Tasso, as both a creator of original poetry in the epic form and a theorist equal to anyone else writing in the century, responded fully to the complex of expectations, cultural associations, and attempted formulations surrounding this most admired of all Renaissance poetic genres. His ideas, in the *Discorsi* and other prose works, reveal that he was inclined to range himself with a Minturno, much more than with a Cintio or Patrizi. I have already pointed up his expression of the ancient position. But here we can see how directly his statements constitute an answer to Cintio (see passage quoted on pp. 27–28).

Tasso deliberately moved the discussion back to the fundamentals which Cintio wanted to evade by his definition of romance. He simply asserts that art is an enduring entity whose forms are based in an eternal nature. The whole idea of a continually varying poetry and poetics has no validity whatsoever. As a necessary consequence, he makes it impossible to define a romance as a long narrative poem with a multiple plot, because unity of plot of some sort is essential to poetic form itself. There can be no work of art which does not embody that principle. Tasso sees the "modern" challenge as basically destructive, rather than creative, in its implications for poetry. Behind his statement lies the delicate balancing of "art," the fundamental disciplined order learned mainly from the reasoning and practice of the classical writers, and "custom," the varying details and surfaces, colors and tones that derive from contemporary tastes, an adjustment which constitutes the major effort of the *Discorsi*. But, Tasso implies, an exclusive dependence on contemporary taste or usage destroys that equilibrium and the fruitful connections with tradition that depend on it. Once art is cut loose from that whole complex of judgments derived from reason and precedent, one can no longer conceive of an ordered, defined concept, "art." Then anything goes. And the element of "disciplina," the restraint, even austerity, implied in Tasso's Aristotelian ideas, becomes meaningless. With that element goes the whole morally essential relationship between the rational order of art and the rational order of nature implied in Tasso's Aristotelianism. The poet cannot be a creator analogous to God, the creator of harmoniously related works and words.

Writing in the epic form, however, opens just such possibilities to the suitably disciplined and inspired poet. Such is the implication of the celebrated passage on the special kind of unity proper to epic, perhaps the most beautiful prose in the *Discorsi*.

> For myself, I consider it [variety] both necessary and possible to achieve in the heroic poem. Just as in this wonderful realm of God, called the world, we see scattered over the sky such a variety of stars, and then descending lower step by step, the air and the sea full of birds and fish; and the earth home of so many animals both wild and tame, with brooks, springs, lakes, meadows, fields, forests and mountains; here fruits and flowers, there ice and snow, here cultivated, inhabited land, there fearsome solitary wastes.—With all this, the world, which encloses in its womb such quantity and diversity of things, is one—one in form and essence and one the way in which its divergent parts, with a harmony made out of disharmony [*discorde concordia*] are joined and bound together. There is nothing lacking in this world and yet there is nothing excessive or unnecessary. Just so I judge that an excellent poet (who is called divine only because he comes to resemble the supreme Artificer by working in similar ways and thus participating in the nature of divinity) should make [*formar*] a poem, in which, as in a small world, we read here about the movements of armies, land and sea battles here, conquests of cities, skirmishes and duels, jousts, there descriptions of hunger and thirst, here storms, there fires, or monstrous appearances; there we see celestial and infernal councils, mutinies, conflicts, wanderings, adventures, enchantments, deeds of cruelty, daring, courtesy, generosity, the vicissitudes of happy or unhappy love, now joyous, now pathetic. Nevertheless the poem, containing such variety of matter, is one, one in form and fable [*favola*] and all these things are put together in such a way that each element is related to the other, each corresponds to the other, and each element depends on the other either by necessity or verisimilitude, so that if only one part were removed or changed its place, the whole would be destroyed. (Pp. 35–36)

The excellent poet's *art*, his ordering and shaping of material, is what gives him his divinity, not the mysterious nature of his powers nor the universality of his concerns. Tasso's stakes in the concept of art become clear. If, as he argues, the "modern" attempt to base poetics on the vicissitudes of contemporary usage, is essentially destructive to "the nature of art," then it destroys what gives enduring value to the poet's work. The poet, the "maker" in the classical designation, can be a creator analogous to the divine, original creator *(il supremo Artefice)*, if he shapes his work so as to correspond to the ordering of God's work. Implied in Tasso's defense and assertion of a rational, perennial poetics is that whole morally essential connection between the order of art and the order of nature.[19]

This passage itself exemplifies such a connection, while stating an idea derived from his Aristotelian premises. The *point* of this elaborate paragraph is a fairly limited one, if essential to Tasso's concept of the epic and to the nature of his actual poem. It is based on that distinction between "simple" and "composite" unity, the language of which I discussed earlier. And Tasso argues the point here in much the same way. He makes the analogy to nature first and with great elaboration. Our assent to the truth of his description of nature is transferred to his literary idea. The metaphor becomes the argument, so intimately does he connect the natural and literary realms.

But in this passage, an almost physical force is generated by the elaboration of the images, the onrush of phrases creating compelling rhythmic patterns, the inclusiveness of the details, the symmetry with which the parallel is expressed (". . . one in form and essence"—"one in form and fable"). And Tasso reinforces this kind of power by the physical structuring that takes place within the natural metaphor and is then transferred, by analogy, to the literary sphere. The order in which he mentions the various elements of "this wonderful realm of God, called the world" actually reproduces verbally the hierarchical structure of physical nature, so essential to the Renaissance sense of order in the world, "the sky . . . and then descending *lower* step by step, the air and the sea . . . and the earth. . . ." In addition, the physical imagery of the line of creation follows the order of the creation story in *Genesis*. Tasso cements the analogy between the creative poet and the works of "the supreme Artificer" with a completeness that assures our conviction. Before the literary point is even argued, the metaphor of nature contains, by implication, a full sense of a physical and moral order created by God, the "maker," an order which should furnish the foundation and ultimate reference for what the poet, the "maker," creates.

The parallels between the ordered details in the description of God's world and the details of that "small world," the epic poem, generate, with that sense of physical power, a feeling of profound and undeniable truth, far beyond what one would expect from a paraphrase of the argument. As the first part of the passage moves from the large entities of heaven, sea, earth to the smaller elements of landscape and organic life, and then suggestions of human details, the second "literary" section begins with the panoramic scene of "movements of armies, land and sea battles," proceeds to the detailing of "conquests of cities, skirmishes and duels, jousts, description of hunger and thirst," and then to the specifics of human action—"conflicts, adventures . . . deeds of cruelty, daring . . . vicissitudes of love." In sum, the wealth of imagery Tasso brings to bear on his relatively simple point about the nature of unity in an epic implicates in his conception of epic unity a vast sense of the natural and moral order to which the "excellent poet" is responsible.

At the same time, he has succeeded in creating an idea of a unified plot inclusive of that element which other critics would lead one to consider its polar opposite, variety. Unity of action seems to be the basic Aristotelian tenet, whose defense separates a rational, immutable poetics from a "modernist" one. But Tasso expands the notion of unity to allow into the epic much of what was most tenaciously defended by critics like Cintio. "Moderns" saw the variety resulting from Ariosto's multiple plot as one of the chief sources of the *Furioso*'s greatness. Tasso succeeds in incorporating just that principle in the concept of unity, which he then proceeds to defend as an essential to genuinely poetic structure. Characteristically, this passage finally creates the most vivid responses to the idea of variety, because of the sheer weight, energy, and intensity of the language used to express it. But the manifest content of the passage controls the assertion of variety by declaring for unity. Tasso rather triumphantly achieves here that disciplined inclusiveness characteristic of his best work. He defends a principle which he considers essential to a rational and moral sense of art. At the same time, he finds a way of understanding that principle that allies him to contemporary (and his own) taste.

This is perhaps the best example of his response to the modern challenge. He completely rejects the principle of basing poetics on contemporary usage. But he defines the "eternal" laws of poetry in such a way that he can include what seems most valuable in contemporary taste. In the end he appears more flexible and inclusive than his antagonists, who felt that they were cutting loose from traditionalist rigidities. Because he rejects the idea of poetics varying with time, he also frees himself from the modernist corollary, that poetics be based on contemporary models rather than on precepts. He can incorporate what he wants from the romances into his idea of epic, while defending his form as one based on an eternal rational and moral order, independent of any purely human example.

This means that, unlike Cintio and Pigna, he would see epic as a form existing outside classical, as well as contemporary, precedent. Both Cintio and Pigna define genres simply as schematic descriptions of specific models. They identify the epic form with classical culture, as they proclaim romance to be particularly Italian. They (especially Pigna) attempt to distinguish epic and romance not only by the unity-multiplicity dichotomy, but by pointing to the difference in the religion used in the poem. That is, they create rather ad hoc definitions of the forms, based on particular models. So epic becomes a poem with a single action based on the classical pagan religion, while romance is a narrative of multiple plot founded on Christianity. Tasso eliminates the basis for such a distinction by insisting on a poetics of precepts, defining forms according to fundamental principles he feels to be derived from nature and reason, in the manner of Aristotle. Epic as a form really exists as independently of specific classical as of contemporary models, though classical precedent does carry a great deal of weight in determining its proper attributes. The poet enjoys, in fairly large measure, the freedom to adapt and shape his form, within the essential Aristotelian foundation.

That he has cleared a freer path than seems proper to the strictest classicists is evident in something like his letter to one member of that group of "revisers," to whom he sent his manuscript, canto by canto. In this letter, he defends the specific sorts of variety included in the *Gerusalemme* against the essentially moral and religious criticisms of his correspondent, Silvio Antoniano, a man of whose "excessive severity" he complained to others.[20] The debate centers on two elements of variety—the marvels interspersed through the poem, and particularly the whole complex of love episodes. But Tasso mobilizes primarily literary defenses. They demonstrate, in specific terms, what he means by unity achieved

out of variety. He is concerned to show that what looks
supererogatory to Antoniano is actually essential to the poem's
unity, on the one hand, and, more defensively, does not violate
any basic principle of epic poetry.

He starts by confessing:

> It is certainly true that the enchantments of Armida's garden and of
> the forest, and the loves of Armida, Erminia, Rinaldo, Tancredi and
> the others, are aspects of the poem that I could not cut out without
> any, or at least without obvious, deficiency in the totality of the work.

Though at first he defends such episodes, and some of the imper-
fections of character in his heroes, by citing the indications for
such situations in the historical sources, he urges his main defenses
on the grounds of what is proper for the epic poem. In the case of
the marvels:

> In my judgment it is very necessary that any heroic poem include the
> marvelous, that which goes beyond the usual action and even beyond
> human possibility, whether it be presented as the power of the gods as
> in the poems of the pagans, or as the power of angels, devils, and
> magicians as in all modern poetry.

He argues that this difference from ancient precedent should not
be criticized, because it concerns the accidents rather than the
essentials of poetry. What is essential is the presence and effectiveness of the superhuman, the "marvelous;" and the specific machinery by which this is achieved depends, properly, on cultural
variation. In such "accidents," he goes on to declare, Homer is not
the law. Instead, he states very clearly his own definite understanding of the relationship between eternal law and individual
variety and adaptation:

> Nor do I attribute to him [Homer] full authority over poetry, as
> many do; in my judgment there are certain things attributed to him
> that are really *sui juris:* people cite him to defend the laws of poetry,
> which are essential and fixed by the very nature and law of things (such
> as the prescription of unity of action and some other similar things);
> but in those accidents in which one does not and cannot prescribe a
> fixed rule for the poet, it is not inappropriate, in my judgment, to go
> quite far from the imitation of the ancients, as it is perhaps superstition
> to seek to imitate them in every aspect. It seems to me that Aristotle

teaches us this quite openly in the Rhetoric and the Poetics, by keeping silent; for he shows us that he considers those things about which he is silent to be aspects of writing which cannot be defined by any norm of art.

This reveals his basic defense of those differences from classical example in his poem that had been criticized using Homer especially as a legislating authority. With a typical, if minor, irony, he supports his declaration of independence from such authority by citing the authority of Aristotle. He applies this reasoning also to the love episodes in the poem, though he can cite precedent for those, too, in Virgil and Apollonius.

In addition, he finds it necessary to justify the importance given to Rinaldo, when he has made Goffredo the "hero" of the poem in the strict sense, and has also insisted on unity of action. His arguments seem rather forced, but are interesting, in part for that very reason. They demonstrate how important such ideas looked to Tasso, even if they did not provide the soundest defense for his practice. In the first place, he again uses a "natural" metaphor as an argument. He declares that no matter how much importance is given to Rinaldo, the poem is still unified because of the natural hierarchy of the relationship between the two heroes. Goffredo is Rinaldo's superior; Rinaldo is the instrument, the executor of Goffredo's ideas. They are related organically as the head (or heart) is to the arm.[21] As members of one body, they present a basically unified protagonist. In the second place, he urges as a defense the nature of the audience to which he directs his poem. He is not writing, he says, just to the learned ("nor am I content to write to a select few, even if Plato were among them.") Rather he wants to appeal to contemporary men in general. Therefore, he needs "variety and grace [vaghezza], neither of which is found [by contemporaries] in the ancient poems." Such variety and grace cannot be achieved in this poem without Rinaldo and the episodes dependent on him.

This is a much more defensive argument for variety than the long passage in the Discorsi, though such defensiveness can be explained by the context in which it was written. But it does offer us a clue to Tasso's conception of the audience he desires for his poem. This, too, causes him to seek greater freedom within the limits created by classical tradition and precedent. His adaptations of romance material cannot be attributed solely to the vaguely romantic, expansionist and antiauthoritarian longings usually cited as the source of his divergences from strict interpretation of classicist precepts.

We need to understand more completely what kind of audience Tasso envisions, however, since it is an important way of illuminating his interpretation of the available precedents and their appropriate adaptation to his own poetic structure. He does not really conceive of the same audience as Cintio, the audience of contemporaries which seems to demand the cultivation of popular styles. The whole moral and intellectual orientation of *Discorsi* obviously precludes such a simple idea of the audience. The people to whom he first sent his poem were of the "few," the men of soundly moral judgment, who could be expected to take "pleasure" from what satisfies the demands of order, morality, and tradition. Nevertheless, Tasso constantly talks about the necessity for "delight," for "grace," and cites the demands of the audience as his justification. He ends up with no very precise delimitation of his audience. This is perfectly appropriate to his idea of the epic. The grandest, most encompassing and far-reaching poetic form, the "small world" created by a poet operating on the vastest scale possible for the human imagination, should appeal to all that is worthwhile in human society. So in a letter to Scipione Gonzaga of July, 1575:

> I never proposed to please the stupid mob; but, on the other hand, I would not want to satisfy only experts and connoisseurs [*i maestri de l'arte*]. I am truly most desirous of the applause of average men [*uomini mediocri*]; I seek the good opinion of such people as much as that of the more knowledgeable. Therefore I ask your Highness what you can learn of the reactions of the refined people at court [*cortigiani galanti*] and of average men.[22]

To justify his attention to the "delight" produced by his poem, Tasso uses his legitimate desire to appeal to the *"uomo mediocre,"* that favorite Renaissance phrase for the man who embodies the "mean," the middle way in all the human potential for good and evil. But his rejection of Cintio's search for a purely contemporary poetics would seem to imply at least a partial redefinition of pleasure, and a rather more complex moral attitude toward it. The audience's need for pleasure in literature may justify those qualities or situations in his poem which are more effectively productive of delight than of moral instruction. Yet the tone of such an argument, especially in something like the letter to Antoniano is quite defensive, as though Tasso himself suspects that there is something questionable about the pleasure created by imaginative literature. One need only remember the elaborate defense of poetry which Bernardo Tasso felt it necessary to write to sense Tasso's absorption of the condemning attitudes toward such pleasure prevalent in the critical milieu of the century. The Platonic, the ultra-Catholic, the severely moralistic attacks on poetry were perfectly well known to him.[23] They influence the assumptions on which his theory is based. In relation to his specific literary problems, this moral devaluation of the element of delight needed by his audience means that the audience itself becomes a temptation. What the audience wants and what he must achieve to find favor with it is a kind of literature whose moral value he himself questions (hence the defensiveness of tone in response to criticisms along these lines). More specifically, romance, romance material, characters, techniques, or effects, are suspect. That form not only seems based on a poetics that divorces literature from the moral foundation of natural order and law, but seems to do so for the sake of the most ephemeral kind of pleasure.

To further complicate the problem, Tasso could not simply advocate imitation of the Greek and Roman epics admired by learned readers. Though the classical poems provided him with his only real examples of the epic, they express a pagan culture. For Tasso and his audience, Christians in a period when true Christianity was being defined more and more exclusively, the pre-Christian cosmos and ethos of classical epic seriously undermined its value. In his theory, Tasso was able to include the classical models as embodiments of aesthetic principles whose moral connotations made them not only correct but right. In the poem, he explores the potentiality for contradiction in his simultaneous reverence for classical art and rejection of pagan moral and religious values. In addition to Ariostan romance, he presents classical poetry ambivalently as the "soavi licor" (sweet syrups) disguising the life-giving medicine of Christian truth.

Nevertheless, the dilemma was not, at least for the early Tasso, totally polarized. He was not really forced to fall between two irreconcilable goals for literature, pleasure and morality. In fact, the struggle to include all the varieties of tradition, to appeal to the whole audience, led him to some of his most fruitful choices. Since he insists that he wants to be read by everyone, he has to confront directly the fact that romance, especially romance as exemplified by Ariosto and analyzed by Cintio, represents the genuinely popular vein of narrative poetry in his time. If he wants to be considered a great poet by the "cortigiani galanti" with whom he spent most of his life, and by literate people in general, he must find some accommodation with this kind of literature.

More significantly, he himself responded with great intensity to the imaginative qualities of romance material. Romance seemed to allow scope for the emotional and sensuous responses to experience that formed so large a part of Tasso's poetic sensibility. Romance's merging of formal boundaries, the combinations of tones and moods, expressed objectively in the variety of subjects and characters, powerfully attracted this writer whose tastes led him to lyric contemplation, to introspective or sensual description, as well as to objective, strictly limited narrative movement. Tasso's unwillingness actually to sacrifice the essentials of either pole reveals the power of both sides in this dilemma. As a poet, he responds to the individualist, varied, emotionally appealing strands of romance with an intensity equal to his feeling for the qualities of a more classic form, the discipline and controlled grandeur derived from literary tradition and moral authority. Therefore, as theorist and critic, he finds infinite ways of achieving a *via media*.

His assimilation of contemporary models, as well as strictly theoretical ideas, exemplifies this fundamental path of compromise. He explicitly acknowledges the influence of two sixteenth-century poets, Trissino and his father, Bernardo Tasso. They represent not only models for the dual role of poet-theoretician, but practitioners of that specific form with which he is primarily concerned for his whole creative life. They both attempted to solve the same literary—moral problems presented to Torquato Tasso by the epic as a genre. His judgments on their performance and use of their example demonstrate the kind of literary self-education that underlies both the *Discorsi* and the *Gerusalemme*. Both the *Italia liberata* and the *Amadigi* offered him essential exercises in practical criticism. They seem almost as important to him in some ways as his absorption of the Greek and Roman classics. In the work of these immediate predecessors he could survey concrete examples of the epic as a Christian and contemporary form. His analysis of them pushed him to formulate the boundaries and contours of his own poetic territory. The influence of his thought about these contemporaries emerges as early as the *Rinaldo*, his first complete narrative, written at the age of eighteen. But the title alone indicates how much Trissino survived in Tasso's mind when he came to write his great poem. *La Gerusalemme liberata* clearly recalls *L'Italia liberata;* while the difference in proper nouns comes to symbolize a great deal of the difference in the structure Tasso built on his literary foundation.

Before considering these two acknowledged precursors in more detail, it is illuminating to speculate briefly about the most significant absence in Tasso's indication of models for Christian epic—the *Divina commedia*.[24] Despite contemporary controversy over the genre and worth of Dante's poem,[25] it would appear to compel attention as the major Christian narrative on an epic scale in Italian. But Dante's figurative mode was closed to Tasso. Though, in his poem, he acknowledges the *Commedia* as a significant predecessor by local imitation and allusion, his understanding of the poet's role and the nature of poetry differs from Dante's in important ways. Dante designed his figurative structure and language to pierce the veil concealing the ultimate realities of our existence. In the *Commedia*, he insists on the divine origins of his vision. By God's grace, he tells us, he went on his journey and saw the eternal pain of Inferno, the stages of purification in Purgatorio, and the ever-growing radiance of divine love in Paradiso. The poem is a *retelling*, a recalling to memory of his vision, so as to stimulate an analogous vision in us.

> Ahi quanto a dir qual era è cosa dura
> esta selva selvaggia e aspra e forte
> che nel pensier rinova la paura!
>
> *Inferno*, I, 4–6

Ah, how hard it is to tell what that wood was, wild, rugged, harsh; the very thought of it renews the fear!

> Io non so ben ridir com'i'v'intrai.
>
> I, 10

I cannot rightly say how I entered it.

> e io sol uno
> m'apparecchiava a sostener la guerra
> sì del cammino e sì de la pietate,
> che retrarrà la mente che non erra.
> O Muse, o alto ingegno, or m'aiutate;
> o mente che scrivesti ciò ch'io vidi,
> qui si parrà la tua nobilitate.
>
> II, 3–9

and I alone was making ready to sustain the strife, both of the journey
and of the pity, which unerring memory shall retrace. O Muses, O
high genius, help me now! O memory that wrote down what I saw,
here shall your worthiness appear![26]

When he calls on the Muses, on "alto ingegno," he is calling on
divine power that transcends his own unaided capacity. His nobility appears in his ability to remember and translate into language
"ciò ch'io vidi." The emphasis lies on the objective truth of his
vision.[27] Poetic, i.e., allegorical, language is the necessary vehicle
to render comprehensible to the rest of us "things invisible to
mortal sight." The poet claims to invent nothing. His genius consists in the fact of vision, first of all, and secondly in his capacity to
retell effectively what he saw, literally to make it visible to us
through the medium of words, just as God offers his Revelation
through the Word (Scripture). Such a view depends on the belief,
persistent through, but rarely beyond, the Renaissance, in "both
the objective reality of an invisible realm and a required relation
between that realm and the realities perceived by sense."[28]

Tasso expresses a problematic relation to this older understanding of poet and poem. The *Discorsi* clearly embody what became
the usual neoclassical theory.[29] In that text, the poet is maker, not
seer. God is "il supremo Artefice" and the poet is divine in his
capacity to invent and order a "piccolo mondo". All Tasso's interest in subject matter centers on selection, choice, whereas for
Dante the subject is chosen by divine grace. Tasso does imply that
subjects objectively contain within them certain inevitable attributes. But the attributes that concern him relate not to ineffable
mystery needing translation into apprehensible terms, but to literary technique—appropriateness to the chosen genre or style, effect
on the audience, suitability to poetic invention. Significantly, the
major portion of the *Discorsi* deals with "disposition"—ordering
the work of the master craftsman. The kind of truth to which he
pays most attention is verisimilitude, a conviction of truth in the
audience to be achieved through a historical subject and a treatment of that subject essentially in accord with "nature." If he
insists on the analogy between nature and the poet's world, it is an
analogy to rational nature, comprehensible by most intelligent,
reasonably educated people. He defines poetry as mimetic, dependent on nature, rather than transcendent, dependent on divine
revelation.

But in the *Gerusalemme liberata*, the poet assumes a more complicated stance. The Platonic vein in Tasso's thought expands and

suggests the possibility of transcendent vision. The Platonism (or better, Neoplatonism) of the *Discorsi* consists primarily in the triumphant resolution of the unity-multiplicity conflict through the aesthetic principle of *discordia concors*. Tasso exploits this idea in ways that seem totally compatible with his neoclassical emphasis on the integrity of the poem as an aesthetic object and on poetic invention. But the poem reaches beyond the "piccolo mondo" of rational nature and historical experience. Tasso opens it to the mysterious and transcendent through his "meraviglioso." Epic must reveal the super-natural, the extra-ordinary, and connect them to temporal mortal life. Tasso works for such revelation of mystery and transcendent connection in his re-creation of romantic wonder and in the prophetic or biblical visions. Despite the coherently rational adherence to nature advocated in the *Discorsi*, poetic power clearly stems as much from the expression of purely visionary or imagined experience. Imagination, for him, can still imply, as it did for earlier poets, the vision of an ideal, invisible reality. The poet's images can be both visionary and mimetic, because he imitates the extra-ordinary, the divine order not ordinarily apprehensible by sense or even reason. In fact, epic grandeur eludes the strict adherent of neoclassical sense, as Tasso indicates in his discussion of Trissino. By expanding his poetry to imagined spaces on earth beyond the Pillars of Hercules or in the enchanted core of forests and to divine heights and infernal depths above and below earth, he seeks a transcendence of temporal and physical limitation. He works to embody persuasively the Neoplatonic vision of the divine (and infernal) capacities in humans, operating through history but ultimately precipitating them beyond it.[30] But what he achieves paradoxically is the transformation of historical experience into the psychological and moral that is, effectively, a powerful movement inward in narrative poetry.

Unlike Dante's, his claims to perceive such truth of the interior life through divine revelation remain problematic. Imaginative truths, perceived, as they must be, through deliberate fictions, the poet's inventions, suffer the strains of doubt, though not yet disbelief. To an eighteenth-century poet like Collins, for whom rationalizing skepticism has largely undermined the visionary claims of poetry, Tasso appears to enjoy the "undoubting mind [that] believ'd the magic wonders which he sung."[31] But Tasso felt it necessary to apologize for the "fregi" (ornaments) with which he sees himself embellishing the historical, theological truth. His attitude to the romantic and visionary dimensions of his poem ex-

presses strain, if not division, in his relation to his own tradition.[32]
His neoclassical definitions of epic, in practice, come into conflict
with the movement to ideal orders of reality pursued whole-
heartedly in Dante's imagining of the soul's life.

Tasso's more immediate predecessors, like Trissino and Bernardo Tasso, offered him models for Christian epic both potentially surpassable and yet more closely comparable in conception
to his own thinking. Trissino's poem certainly reflects the theoretical ideas he formulated in his *Poetica*. There he had criticized the
Orlando furioso for being written merely to please the crowd. He
insisted, instead, on the serious educative mission of the poet and
on the necessity for historical erudition, because poetry should
preserve truth. The poem he actually wrote, *L'Italia liberata dai
goti,* could hardly instruct more explicitly nor offer more loyal
faith to history. With pedantic thoroughness, Trissino applied the
carefully elaborated rules for epic poems he thought he had derived
directly from classical practice. His verse is unrhymed and non-
stanzaic, thus immediately divorced from the techniques of
versification that characterize romances. The poem attempts to
recount the whole history of the liberation of Italy under Justin-
ian, while adhering strictly to Aristotelian canons of unity and
Christian ideas of moral purity and pious religion.

The poetic qualities of the invocation summarize the main attributes of this poem as a model for a strictly correct Aristotelian
epic. The poet calls on "Divine Apollo and You celestial Muses"
(I, 1),[33] the proper classical references for an epic poem. But the
supernatural machinery with which the poem opens involves the
Christian God and the angels. Trissino is enough a man of the
earlier Renaissance to feel no conflict in this combination. These
classical divinities, however, are those "Ch'avete in guardia i
gloriosi fatti, / E i bei pensier de le *terrene* menti" (Who protect the
glorious deeds and beautiful thoughts of *earthly* minds, I, 2–3).
The real actors in the poem are God, to whom Trissino refers with
the culturally general periphrasis of "L'altissimo Signor, che il ciel
governa" (The highest Lord, who rules heaven, I, 15), the angels,
and allegorical personifications of Christian ideas like "Providenza" (I, 18).

The poet states the subject directly, and immediately launches
the plot on its way with a dialogue set in heaven.

> Piacciavi di cantar per la mia lingua,
> Come quel Giusto, ch'ordinò le leggi,

Tolse a l'Italia il grave, e aspro giogo
Degli empi Goti, che l'avean tenuta
In dura servitù presso a cent'anni:
Per la cui libertà fù molta guerra;
Molto sangue si sparse; e molta gente
Passò nanzi'l suo dì ne l'altra vita,
Come permesse la divina altezza:
Ma dite la cagion, che'l mosse prima
A far sì bella, e gloriosa impresa.
L'altissimo Signor, che il ciel governa,
Si stava un dì fra le beate genti,
Riguardando i negozi de' mortali;
Quando un'alma virtù, che Providenza
Da noi si chiama, sospirando disse:
O caro Padre mio, da cui dipende
Ogni opra, chi si fà là giuso in terra,
Non vi muove pietà? quando mirate,
Che la misera Italia già tant'anni
Vive suggetta ne la man de' Goti?

(I, 1–21)

May it please you to sing through my voice
How that Just one, who codified the laws,
Removed from Italy the heavy, harsh yoke
Of the impious Goths, who had held her
In hard servitude for almost a hundred years.
There was much warfare for that liberty;
Much blood was shed, and many people
Passed over to the other life before their time
As divine greatness permitted.
But first relate the cause that first moved him
To undertake such a beautiful and glorious enterprise.
The highest Lord, who rules heaven
Looked down, from among the blessed folk
On the activities of mortal men.
One sustaining power, called Providence
By us, spoke sighing:
O my dear Father, on whom depends
Every work done down there on earth,
Are you not moved to pity when you
See that miserable Italy has lived
For so many years subject in the hands of the Goths?

If nothing else, this passage provides a model for direct, limited, prosaic poetic discourse. If one compares it to the involuted syntax and rich imagery of Tasso's "ottave," it sounds like plain talk, despite the few mild periphrases and direct classical references. Trissino provides a fully developed example of a narrative poem with a limited, sequential plot, based on authoritative historical material, clear-cut moral stance, and unadorned, almost prosaic style—in short a fully realized, concrete picture of one set of the polarities in the theoretical debate.

Tasso self-consciously assessed the relationship between his own *Liberata* and the earlier one. But he did not criticize Trissino's epic simply because of its relative unpopularity, due to a too strict Aristotelianism. He also seemed to feel that he had achieved better what Trissino was striving for, a coherent poem on a serious, historical theme. Yet he too found himself reinterpreting and pushing open the discipline of their common classical models. Thus in a letter to Orazio Capponi of July 1576:

> The episodes in the *Italia liberata* are perhaps looser than those of my Goffredo, and they are less integrated with the plot and less dependent on it. Moreover, I undertake to sing only of what was done, after six years of war, during 3 or 4 months in the conquest of Jerusalem, and I attempt to tie it all together, so that there is no doubt about the unity of the action. . . . But Trissino sings of the entire war fought for the liberation of Italy; therefore he has not only the action around Rome, but in all of Italy, with conquests of many cities. However, I would not be so bold as to say that there are multiple plots, as Sperone and Barga say openly. It seems to me that all the deeds come from one beginning and are directed toward one end, so it is possible to salvage the idea of one action. . . . Nevertheless, I must confess that my plot is somewhat more expansive and composite than that of the Iliad. But if I had directed the action toward any other goal than the conquest of Jerusalem, I would not have been able to achieve as much variety in the episodes as I wanted. . . .[34]

Trissino's poem appears as an abortive attempt to write the poem that was eventually achieved in the *Gerusalemme liberata*.

His own father's *Amadigi* also stimulated Tasso's mind as he worked at the solutions to the formal problems set up by criticism. This poem contrasts with Trissino's, in the first place, because of its success with the courtly audience cultivated by both Tassos. But it also represents a more or less opposing path through the critical dualities involved in writing narrative poetry, for it is basically an Ariostesque romance. Bernardo Tasso responded to the theoretical dilemmas of the time by trying to moralize and domesticate an essentially romantic form and subject matter. Like his son, he cast his verse in the romantic tradition, i.e., in *ottava rima*. But he also extended the story through 100 cantos. The invocation states its subject as "L'eccelse imprese, e gli amorosi affanni / Del Prencipe Amadigi, e d'Oriana" (the high deeds and amorous pains of the Prince Amadis and Oriana, I, 1–2),[35] i.e., the subject matter of romance. But in probably deliberate distinction from the *Orlando furioso*, they are the loves and deeds of one hero and heroine, rather than the potentially rich array of Ariosto's "Lad*ies*, princes," etc. And of course, his muse is a wholly Christian one, the Virgin, called "Holy Mother of Love" (I, 17). His father provides Tasso with a complete example of a "reformed" Ariosto, a romance whose morality and form comes closer to the stricter views of a post-Tridentine milieu.

But as Tasso's judgment on Trissino makes clear, this really cannot satisfy him. He does not want to write romance, but epic. His poem must have a fully realized coherence and unity, achieved with material whose power derives from its essential "truth"; and that means basically historical subject matter. One can see from his early experiments in the *Rinaldo* how completely both these paths are involved in his poetic personality. For even in that extremely youthful work, the examples of both Trissino and Bernardo Tasso have been reworked into a new *via media*. His emotional affinities did draw him to the tradition of vernacular romance. The personal intimacy of this kind of literature, the feeling of intense longing and pleasure that seems associated with romance for him, is appropriately symbolized by the intimacy of his tie to the author of the *Amadigi*. But the intellectual convictions and moral needs associated with the classical epic tradition were equally strong. As early as the *Rinaldo*, he worked to discipline romance material into a more rigorous form.

The preface to this poem represents Tasso's earliest critical writing (1561–62).[36] Its main theme already reflects the effort to reconcile epic and romance. Tasso registers his awareness of the problems of audience-appeal on the one hand, and theoretical acceptability on the other. He also reveals his grand ambitions and thus an attraction to the classically heroic rather than strictly "romantic" tradition. He casts Ariosto in the role of antagonist rather than master, and reserves the unadulterated praise for Homer and Virgil.

It is possible to see him working out these issues in the poem itself, though with less impressive results than he achieves in the *Gerusalemme*. The *Rinaldo* does not display the kind of organic coherence Tasso sought in the *Liberata,* and whose absence he decried in Trissino. Rather, his practical compromise in the debate over unity was to have one hero and multiple actions, linked in a linear way. And he was still working almost completely with standard romance episodes.[37] The characters and plot are highly conventional. Most strikingly the poem reveals an extraordinary literary culture in endless verbal echoes, and in details and larger structures modeled on other poems. But, as Brand has pointed out sympathetically, one must relate this to the overwhelmingly literary quality of Tasso's experience (or inexperience) at this young age.[38]

As a model for Tasso's poetic practice, the *Rinaldo* exemplifies important characteristics of his techniques for creation of a new poem within a given tradition. Though he is clearly moving toward the place within the epic tradition achieved in the *Liberata,* this early poem is much more aligned with the *Amadigi,* than with the *Italia liberata* (rather than incorporating, and transcending them both and what they both represent). But here he already makes his choices on the basis of what appears right to him as a poet, and explains them by an eclectic approach to theoretical problems. He is not burdened down by the weight of Aristotle, Horace, and contemporary theorists. Rather, he adheres most closely to literary sources, to the example of the great poets of the past. At the same time, he obviously deals with those moral and religious pressures, that come to be associated with certain aspects of the contemporary critical climate. His version of the Rinaldo story, like his father's tale of Amadis, reflects a concern for piety, moral discipline, and conformity to standards established by court and church.

The contemporary literary models available to Tasso presented him with alternative poetic models analogous to the polarities debated in theoretical discussions. On the one hand, he sees the *Italia liberata,* a correct, Aristotelian poem determinedly derived from classical culture, yet lacking in genuine relevance to contemporary sensibilities. This model also falls short aesthetically, in the qualities of coherence and organic structure which his own poetic judgment demands. The *Amadigi,* on the other hand, provides him with an emotionally appealing example of the freer, more eccentric, varied vernacular romance, moralized and ordered in directions congenial to his own more rigorous conscience. Yet it still depends on the fantastic subject matter and unregulated form derived from Ariosto. It also troubles him morally, because it is associated with the temptations of seeing literature primarily as a vehicle of pleasure, catering to the deficient reason of fallen humanity. The *Rinaldo,* dependent as it is on literary experience and the example of other poems, demonstrates directly Tasso's instinctive ways of handling such models. He searches for a structure that can incorporate romance material into a more regular, Aristotelian, and organic form, while recapturing the sense of variety and movement that characterizes the romance tradition. The moral implications of his material already occupy the center of his attention. He is concerned with the moral and religious evaluation of essentially romantic characters. He introduces an opposing thematic force into the fantastic world of knight-errantry, just as his efforts at Aristotelian structure coexist with the widely varying form of romantic poems. In effect, the literary predecessors of the *Gerusalemme,* both his own and others' work, summarize in a schematic way the general orientation within the critical dualities of the time, taken in the *Discorsi.*

Discorsi dell' arte poetica—A Primer for La Gerusalemme liberata

WITHIN such complexity of background and implication, the
Discorsi resolve the various issues with great lucidity. The
easy, conversational tone, enhanced by occasional direct gestures
toward the imagined listener ("signor Scipione"), creates no suggestion of conflict or doubt about "the direct road to making
poetry." If these discourses were indeed written "for self-
mastery,"[1] their clarity and coherence demonstrate considerable
success in the effort. They reflect nothing of the tormented,
agitated man of ambiguity, the Tasso of romantic legend or even of
the letters. They take a grandly casual attitude toward the immense
difficulty of reconciling classical and Christian, epic and romance,
the appeal of historical authenticity and the dignity of moral truth.
Tasso handles these essential and deeply problematic issues with
the succinctness of a professional's manual.

> Anyone who proposes to write a heroic poem must pay attention to
> three things: he must choose material fit to receive [atta a ricever in sé]
> that more excellent form that the poet's artifice will attempt to in-
> troduce into it. He must give the material that form; and finally he
> must clothe the material with those elegant ornaments that are appro-
> priate to its nature. Therefore, this discussion will be divided into
> those three headings. . . . (P. 3)

He starts with "la materia nuda," considering it "raw material"
explicitly analogous to that used by artisans in the ordinary sense.

Here he employs the image of a shipbuilder, who must envision the ultimate form of his ship and know what kind of material can most appropriately be molded into that form. The exact language of this last requirement becomes extremely important for any consideration of the relation between theoretical discourse about epic and the actual epic poetry produced. For Tasso repeats his phrase from the opening sentence ("fit to receive") to convey a basic assumption about the process of poetic creation.

> Just as the shipbuilder not only must know what the form of the ship should be, but also must understand what kind of wood is most *fit to receive* that form, so the poet must have skill [*arte*] not only in shaping [*formare*] the material, but also judgment and understanding of the material itself. He must choose material that *by nature has the potentiality for every perfection*. (My italics, p. 3)

The poet as "maker" operates with conscious choice and control at every level. To write a good poem, he must conceptualize first of all the form of the work as a whole. This means that the form is preexistent, and discoverable by the poet's skill and learning. "Skill" and "judgment," well exercised, lead to the embodiment in a new poem of this form, which can be described in theoretical terms and used as the criterion for judgment of any particular epic poem. In addition, the material in itself has certain attributes that make it more or less appropriate for such a form. By choosing to write a particular kind of poetry with a particular subject matter, the poet creates expectations for his poem that must be fulfilled. Both the genre and the subject matter exist as elements of a reality independent of the poet's mind. Tasso compares the raw material of the poet to wax molded by a seal or to materials like marble, gold, or wood shaped by the great sculptors. One can judge the values and connotations inherent in subject matter quite apart from the poet's use of it; and, conversely, the fact that his subject matter bears culturally determined attributes limits and directs the poet's activity.

From the outset Tasso sees himself as the artisan, consciously selecting and shaping for well-conceived ends. The talk of "perfection," and comparison to artists of supreme quality (Phidias or Praxiteles), occur in the context of deliberate application of skill. The complete absence of any reference to "genius," "divine inspiration," "poetic furor" or any of the other Renaissance terms for the semimystical, enigmatic powers of the poet is characteristic of the *Discorsi,* with their matter-of-fact clarity and sense of mastery over the process of creation. The production of the epic poem takes place, as filtered through this work, on a plane of rationality and sanity. What Tasso outlines here are the demands of reason, of "disciplina" on the practicing poet.

Nevertheless, the well-articulated steps of his reasoning lead him to choices that allow him to include in his conception of epic the preferences created by sensibility and emotional affinity. His final characterization of the raw material most capable of "receiving" the epic form is an excellent example of this process. He bases most of his argument on the necessity for verisimilitude in the epic. Yet he introduces this idea almost parenthetically, as an assumption requiring no defense, to support his choice between imaginary *(finta)* and historical material (p. 4). Verisimilitude is necessary for the epic poem to achieve its end, that readers experience the delight of intense emotional response. Tasso assumes that his poem will fail unless readers can, in reason, feel that the poem's subject matter carries the weight of truth.[2] He registers a shift in the cultural conventions governing his readers' responses to poetic fictions. As in France and England a generation or two later, the ambiguous epistemological status of fictional stories began to cause acute discomfort in the later sixteenth-century Italian audience.

Tasso, like many contemporaries and more successors, attempts to resolve the problem of "truth" in epic narrative by urging its foundation in history, "what truly happened."[3] He understands that general cultural expectations, the common sense of reasonable men, demand historical validity if a poem about "high enterprise" is to appear "verisimilar" *(verisimile).*

> It is not verisimilar that an illustrious action, such as the actions de-
> scribed in a heroic poem, would not be written down and passed on to
> the memory of succeeding ages by some history. *Great events cannot
> be unknown;* if events are not known through some written account,
> from this alone, men will argue that they are false; and believing them
> false will not be so easily moved to anger, fear, pity . . . etc. (My
> italics; pp. 4–5)

Because the genre by definition has to do with "great events," the poet must take into account his audience's assumptions about such events. His sense of contemporary decorum will modulate the poem he visualizes through his knowledge of literary tradition.

The argument for historical subject matter intermingles, with no sense of strain or confusion, reasoning based on aesthetic first principles, on literary tradition, and on assumptions about the contemporary audience, the three major sources of external demands on the poet's individual creation acknowledged by Tasso. But in this basic choice of subject matter, he seems particularly attuned to the expectations created by the traditions of the form and by his sense of his audience's capacities. For instance, an analysis of audience response underlies his insistence that a plot taken from known history creates greater verisimilitude for the poem; an invented story would be considered "false," and a historical one "true." In this context, he seems to argue for the poet's conscious manipulation, even deception, of the audience, in the manner of the classical treatises on rhetoric. In fact, the relation between poet and orator is clearly on his mind, as he had been considering it several paragraphs before. The poet wants to create emotional responses in his readers. For this, the reader must feel that the events with which he becomes involved are "true to life." Tasso presents the historicity of the plot as the best device to achieve this effect.

Tasso's language here is echoed in other contexts with rather different connotations. During the sixteenth century the issue of truth or falsehood could be considered a moral problem, more than a problem of artistic effects on an audience (this is the case in Bernardo Tasso's *Ragionamento della poesia*). In the actual writing of the *Gerusalemme*, Tasso himself clearly understands the relation between a true subject matter and poetic invention to be a moral problem, with the imagined aspects of the poem requiring defense. In his invocation, he begs the Virgin to excuse the "other delights," the "poetic adornments" of the plain truth in the narrative. The choice of proper subject matter becomes a moral choice. The poem's basis in history, its "truth," makes it good, morally right, even a pious act, and one appealing to reason and the cultivated sensibilities of the learned.

Tasso unfolds this implication of the issue quite explicitly in his later, more polemically motivated writing about epic poetry, particularly in his defenses of his own poem. He clearly demonstrates the inherent moral issues in his public statements about the revised version of his poem, *La Gerusalemme conquistata*. For instance, in his defense of the revision, the *Del Giudizio sovra la Gerusalemme di Torquato Tasso da lui medesimo riformata*,[4] Tasso insists on the "truth" of the poem as a moral defense, and justifies the nonhistorical aspects by claiming allegorical meanings for them. Rather than

starting from the problem of popular appeal and implying that the
poet uses historicity to create a necessary conviction of
verisimilitude in his readers, he stresses the poem's exposition of
historical truth and Christian doctrine, and the resultant appeal to
the learned.

In the early *Discorsi,* however, Tasso does not develop the
possibility of moral conflict in the language he accepts as proper to
set an epic poem in relation to a publicly acknowledged reality.
Rather, that tone of the professional's manual, the simple assumption that the enterprise is valuable in itself, leads to an almost
technical treatment of problems that, in the actual production of an
epic, turn out to be as much moral and psychological as aesthetic
for Tasso. The issue in the *Discorsi* is how to achieve perfection in
the genre. Perfection includes appeal to that audience of average
men, whom he explicitly postulates as readers later on.[5] Therefore
he chooses, from the whole array of raw material available to a
poet, a historical subject matter for heroic poetry, because that
would seem verisimilar to the general sense of his audience.
Verisimilitude is also essential because poetry, according to Aristotle, is imitation, that is, "to make similar" *(far simile)* (p. 7).

Such reasoning also justifies him in the choice of a Christian
subject. To a Christian audience, the supernatural elements of an
epic poem could only be convincing if they are based on the Christian religion. Tradition dictates that the world of the poem include
the element of the "marvelous." An epic, in its abstract, ideal
form, consists of elements from both mortal and supernatural life.
To be perfect, the poem has to incorporate that "marvelous." But
the audience for epic has changed in the course of time, so that the
earlier *exempla* of the form cannot be considered the "authority"
that would lead the poet to perfection in any new creation. Christianity introduces an element radically different from ancient epic
into contemporary thinking about the form. Any poem that depends on the classical deities and mythic beings immediately loses
its hold on readers to whom that whole mythology is false.

> A poem that has no marvels is hardly delightful, since marvels move
> the spirit not only of the ignorant, but also of the discriminating. . . .
> But since these miracles cannot occur through any natural power [*virtù
> naturale*] they must be ascribed to some supernatural power; ascribing
> them to the pagan gods immediately destroys verisimilitude, because
> nothing can seem verisimilar to people of our time that they consider

not only false, but impossible. And it is impossible that from such empty, insubstantial idols, that do not exist and never existed, could come things that so much surpass nature and humanity. As for that marvelous (if it is worthy of the name) that goes with the Joves, Apollos and other pagan gods, it is not only far from anything resembling verisimilitude, but is also cold, insipid and without power to move. Anyone of average judgment can see this simply by reading those poems based on the falsehood of ancient religion. (P. 6)

In the dimension of the marvelous, Tasso claims, the classical epics arouse neither excitement nor even interest. A contemporary creator of marvels should actually avoid their example. The kind of freedom Tasso achieves by working at a poetics of precepts rather than of models emerges here. Within the essential principles he can formulate prescriptions for epic in accordance with his own needs. Only a subject from Christian history ensures the high seriousness, the moral orientation, the sense of conformity to an austere, virtuous order that he longs to create in an epic. Therefore, he does not rely on classical models to sanction his choices. Instead he argues from the nature of his audience, in combination with deductions from general Aristotelian precepts about poetry.

He is also able to reconcile what look like opposing elements in epic tradition, the "verisimilar" and the "marvelous." By attributing the supernatural occurrences to God, the angels, devils and other figures believed by Christians to possess miraculous powers, the poet can write a poem that contains both elements and yet never sacrifices verisimilitude.

These deeds, considered in themselves would be called marvels, or even miracles in common speech. But these same deeds can be considered verisimilar if one takes into account the efficacy [*virtù*] and power [*potenza*] of those beings that have accomplished them. . . . (P. 7)

Again, Tasso attends primarily to the characteristics of a contemporary audience. It would be worthless to try to construct a classical epic in a modern language. For the poet to move his readers as intensely and completely as he should, he must appeal to their most deeply rooted beliefs. Any poem that places itself outside this intimately felt area of their experience remains "cold" and "insipid," as well as deficient in verisimilitude.

Tasso rather subtly adjusts an awareness of historical change to

his own conviction of the permanence of artistic principles. He
would agree with Cintio's argument that a mere Italian version of
ancient epic, complete with all the trappings of Greek or Latin
culture, would hardly be relevant to a contemporary audience. But
an adjustment to changing times and readers does not demand a
wholly new form of poetry. Rather, the archetypal form, known
through ancient tradition and precept, must be embodied within
an appropriate cultural framework. This means to him that the
subject matter, not the form, changes. He insists particularly on
the falsehood of classical religion and consequent impotence of the
literary conventions derived from it. Tasso reveres classical culture
selectively, remaining continually aware of the possibilities for total condemnation of any literary allegiance to non-Christian traditions in the post-Tridentine zeal of the sixteenth century. Also, in
keeping with the more sophisticated sensibility of the late Renaissance, he senses a weary pedantry in attempts to make authentic
Italian versions of classical forms. When he relates the story of his
father's first strictly classicist attempt to write a narrative poem
that ended up driving all the courtiers from the hall, he reflects this
development in Italian culture.

A Christian subject for narrative poetry expands the possibilities
of the form to include the tradition hitherto embodied in romance,
while keeping faith with his sense of the eternal order in art. Tasso
arrives at this characterization of the raw material most capable of
being shaped into the perfect heroic poem by a typically eclectic
route. He bases his argument principally on Aristotelian distinctions. This firmly anchors a poem created according to those precepts within the moral framework that makes poetic order
analogous to natural order. By relying on the unchanging forms of
heroic poetry he would assure for any particular new poem the
grandeur, dignity, and seriousness provided through association
with classical tradition in a Renaissance culture saturated with the
assumed value of ancient literature. At the same time, he responds
to the tastes of his own particular audience.

As Tasso further refines his expectations of the proper raw material for the artisan of a heroic structure, he makes inevitable his
actual choices in the *Gerusalemme*. Attuned as he is to the court's
rather precious sense of decorum, he argues for a plot from a
historical period that, in effect, limits the poet to material that had
traditionally been used in romance. If a writer casts about for a
historical subject offering "noble and illustrious events" from a

postclassical period neither so nearly contemporary as to be known in great detail to the living nor so remote as to demand customs that are foreign and therefore unlikely to delight, he almost inevitably comes to the matter of the romances, Arthur or Charlemagne, or to something equally grand from the same general time, i.e., the Crusades.

Tasso clearly intends to set his ideal heroic poem in some relation to romance tradition even before he confronts the issue directly in the second discourse. He continually cites examples from Boiardo and Ariosto as well as from the classics. In characterizing the raw material, as in his more elaborate discussion of unity, he sees his Italian predecessors primarily as antagonists, rather than as models. Nevertheless, he insinuates the idea that epic and romance constitute one tradition, the heroic, long before arguing it directly. He lists examples from famous classical epics and Italian romances as if they were all more or less successful embodiments of the same principles.

Notions of the proper size and shape of epic, derived from Aristotle, also allow him to amalgamate these two previously distinct traditions. The genus "heroic poem" is long, but not so long that men "of average memory" cannot keep the entire plot in mind. "Episodes," that most distinctive feature of the narrative as practiced by Ariosto (also a characteristic of epic in Aristotle), intertwine with and expand the major events. Tasso's solution to these issues, as to the problem of subject matter for the heroic poem, absorbs the culture of the romances. He must then come to terms with the moral and literary traditions associated with those poems, particularly as the conventions are used in the most appealing and, for Tasso, most challenging of them, the *Orlando furioso*. Despite all his negative references to Ariosto's poem, he establishes criteria for a successful heroic poem that necessitate some incorporation of what the *Furioso* represents. In the process he makes inevitable the particularly fruitful tensions created in the *Gerusalemme liberata* by his welding of Christian history and romantic fantasy.

Tasso does attempt to exclude one form of heroic poetry from the theoretical scope of the genre. He firmly distinguishes epic from tragedy, using Aristotelian terminology to disagree with Aristotle. He first summarizes Aristotle's discussion of the issue. According to the *Poetics*, there are three essential differences in genres: the object, manner, and means of imitation. In Aristotle, epic and tragedy differ in manner and means, but not in the objects imitated. They both constitute heroic poetry, because they both imitate "the illustrious." Tasso takes issue with this:

> For these reasons, stated by Aristotle with that obscure brevity characteristic of him, it is generally believed that tragedy and epic are totally alike in the objects of imitation; although this opinion is common and universal, I do not consider it true. . . . (P. 11)

Epic and tragedy cannot, in fact, be based on actions of the same nature because they do not produce the same effects. Tasso argues from the effect on the audience in practice to refute the abstract categorization derived from Aristotle. But he ends by making an equally abstract requirement of epic poetry that imposes considerable limitation on him as the poet of the *Gerusalemme*. He insists that the differing effects of epic and tragedy mean that they, by nature, use different kinds of heroic material. The "illustrious" of epic is not that of tragedy. Tragic actions are designed to arouse pity and terror from sudden reversals within important events. But the nobility in epic depends on exemplary deeds.

> Tragic actions create terror [*orrore*] and pity [*compassione*], and if actions do not arouse terror and pity, they are not tragic. But epics are not born to create pity or terror, nor is this a necessary aspect of epics. If at times heroic poems include some terrible or pitiful situation, nevertheless the whole fabric of the plot is not designed to create terror and pity, and that situation is accidental and simply ornamental. Thus if we call both tragic action and epic action illustrious, they are illustrious in different ways: in tragedy what is illustrious is created by unexpected and sudden change of fortune and by the importance of the events that create terror and pity; but what is illustrious in epic is based on deeds of supreme military power and in deeds of courtesy, generosity, mercy and religion; such deeds, though appropriate to epic, are not at all appropriate to tragedy. (P. 12)

From this, he arrives at an essential difference in the characters appropriate to the two kinds of poetry. The nature of the heroic in tragedy requires characters who are "of regal and supreme dignity," but morally "midway between good and evil." Epic, on the other hand, "needs characters of the height of virtue, who are called heroic because of their heroic virtue." (p. 12) He would demand an uncomplicated idealization of epic characters, so that they can be said to represent some abstract virtue or even the height of all virtues. He is so wedded to this abstract requirement that he would admit the existence of evil by creating characters who "represent" the extreme of evil, rather than accepting the morally ambiguous characterizations of actual life.

Moral criteria should define what is heroic in epic, and select from tradition what can be incorporated unchanged and what must be reshaped for his standard. This theoretical demand for idealization of characters in the context of a subject taken from Christian history leads to some of the most intense and dramatic conflict in the *Gerusalemme*. Yet one would not suspect such a consequence from the rather flat tone of abstract deduction by which Tasso arrives at the idea in the *Discorsi*. He simply considers this aspect of his raw material to be congruent with the other requirements he makes. Within the *Discorsi*, he justifies a moral standard for characterization only by arguing for its logical relation to this particular genre. He carefully remarks that any moral education of readers that might occur is sought by the poet not as poet, but as citizen. As a poet, he seeks to delight by achieving perfection in the genre.

In fact, he sees this demand for an idealized treatment of the material as a way of achieving greater freedom for the poet, especially in the disposition of the poem. He has in mind the distinction between heroic poetry and history. Like Aristotle, he urges the poet's need to adhere to the truth of an idealized concept of human action. The poet owes allegiance not to what was, but to what should be. Though he should found his construction on history, he should shape it to reveal the greatest coherence and logic in events and essential human attributes, qualities never displayed by a retelling of history as it actually occurred (p. 17). Tasso dwells on the artist's freedom to change, to improve history within rather wide limits. He must retain the actual outcome of the "enterprise" and the most well-known events in it, thereby infusing his poem with that authoritative tone derived from a sense of historical validity. Beyond those limits, he is free to, and should, rearrange, expand, reinterpret. He must direct himself toward the goal of "the verisimilar in the universal," truth to the idealized experience of the event as reason would have it.

Tasso's discussion of this issue is brief and matter-of-fact. It has none of the tone of a defense of poetry like his father's or like a later discourse on the art of poetry, Sidney's *Defense*. This argument for poetry's truth to a higher reality was often in the century, and often by Tasso in later writing, used to defend imaginative literature against Christian-Platonic attacks on its falsehood. In the revised *Discorsi,* Tasso exploits this idea heavily to assert the moral and educational value of his poem. When the moral implications of the idea become explicit, it forms part of the self-imposed restriction that Tasso came to exercise in his work on the poem. He moves toward a greater concern for truth and tends to view much of what he included in the poem as extraneous or untrue, requiring defense by allegorical explanation.

But in this earlier version of the *Discorsi,* Tasso holds such implications in solution by his focus on poetry as a value in itself. His reiteration of this idea offers a philosophical justification for poetic license. It opens the door to inclusiveness, so long as the poet has the capacity to shape what he includes into a coherent structure. His matter-of-fact tone suggests that he is not greatly concerned, as a theorist, with the moral difficulties that could result from this allegiance to an idealized version of experience. In practice, the need to imitate actions as they should be in Christian morality or to shape the actions represented so that they come to embody moral ideas, acts as a source of conflict for the poet of the *Gerusalemme liberata.* But within the context of his theory, the concept of a moral and aesthetic idealization of experience is a liberating compromise between the demands of historical validity and the poet's need for imaginative freedom.

Tasso is then free, as a theorist, to turn to a much more elaborate discussion of what he considers essential in the disposition of his subject matter. In the first discourse, under the traditional Horatian category of invention, he gathers his responses to most of the points about epic raised in the *Poetics.* Under the umbrella of disposition, he directly deals with the major issues generated by contemporary theory and practice of heroic poetry. For most of this discourse, he addresses himself to the plot *(la favola).* He cares about three elements, completeness, size, and unity. On each one of these issues he pits his ideal poem against the actuality of the *Furioso* and other romances. So at every turn, he is distinguishing between heroic poems that are mere romances and genuine epic emerging from that tradition.

Tasso devotes by far the major portion of the discourse to the issue of unity. As soon as he mentions it, he sets it in the context of critical controversy with an admirable summary of the essential arguments. His language encourages us to understand the issue as a contest between ancients and moderns, adherents of reason and followers of custom. Its tone converts the controversy into a mock epic itself, with the forces of a popular and vital interloper pitted against a stolid, respectable and dull "establishment."

> Unity of action, signor Scipione, is that topic which has given to our times occasion for long and varied contests among those "led to war by literary fury." For some have considered unity necessary; others have thought multiplicity of action to be more appropriate to a heroic poem, "and everyone considers himself a great judge." The defenders of unity take as their shield the authority of Aristotle, and the majesty of the ancient Greek and Latin poets, nor do they lack the arms given by reason. Their adversaries are the habitual practice [*l'uso*] of present times, the universal agreement of ladies, knights and courts, and, it seems, experience itself, the infallible touchstone of truth; for we see that Ariosto, who departs from the path of ancient writers and from the rules of Aristotle, and has managed to embrace many, diverse actions in his poem, is read and reread by all generations, by both sexes, is known to speakers of all languages, pleases everyone, is praised by everyone, lives in ever-renewed fame, and flies gloriously in the tongues of mortals. On the other hand, Trissino, who proposed to imitate the Homeric poems religiously and restricted himself within the precepts of Aristotle, is mentioned by few people, read by fewer, valued by almost no one, is mute in the theater of the world and dead to the light of men, barely exists buried in libraries or in the study of some scholar. (Pp. 22–23)

But we quickly learn that the sprightly language represents his gesture of tribute to "the divine Ariosto" before throwing down the gauntlet quite definitively on his own.

He proffers a summary of the "modern" arguments he considers worthy of attention. These turn out to be the main points in Cintio's defense of romance as a distinct genre. With these points established as a backdrop, he begins his own elaborate defense of unity of action. This will provide him with his major key to the mediating and thus inclusive position that he wants to occupy in the heroic tradition.

In his first volley against the modernizers, he refutes their fundamental premise. According to Tasso, epic and romance are not and cannot be of distinct species. He proves this by reference to Aristotle's method for distinguishing categories in poetry, specifying the object, manner, and means of imitation. As a result of this analysis he insists that epic and romance must be classed together and judged by the same criteria. Unity of action is an absolute necessity in any poem if it is to be a work of art, with the clearly defined boundaries so essential to the Renaissance sense of form.

He refutes with care and considerable vigor the argument that a
modern heroic poem should be modeled on existing Italian romances and constructed with multiplicity of action, because such is
the custom of the times. Granting that some aspects of human
experience do and should vary with time, he insists that others are
based on principles as eternal as the order of nature. In particular,
beauty exists as a fixed element in nature. Like nature's unvarying
goodness in its adherence to the laws established for it at creation,
the essence of art, an imitation of nature, never changes. What was
once beautiful and good always remains so (p. 33).

With this allegiance to a "fixed and certain" art established, he
creates the basis for a reconciliation of classical epic and modern
romance by distinguishing between essence and accidents in art.
Using this Aristotelian method of reasoning, he arrives at a classic
statement of the position in the heroic tradition that he seeks to fill.
It is founded on the rationally conceived solidity and power of the
classical epics and yet achieves the elegance and attraction of Ariostan romance (pp. 33–34). By creating a structure modeled on classical epic, Tasso expects to ensure "solidity and verisimilitude."
He explicitly associates the issue of unity and adherence to the
example of ancient epics with the whole complex of problems
related to verisimilitude, historical and rational validity, and a solid
conviction of the poem's authority. To construct a poem that truly
imitates nature in its lawfulness and adherence to rational principles requires an allegiance to the classical tradition in the essentials
of art. Moreover, as Tasso developed his ideas in the first discourse, effective application of those principles, especially the
principle of verisimilitude, leads the poet inevitably to a Christian
subject and to a general idealization of character and action. As a
result, the unified poem on a Christian subject seeking solidity and
verisimilitude implies in its very structure a moral and religious
orientation for the development of its material. The power of ancient heroic poetry and of a successful modern poem modeled on it
lies in its capacity to satisfy the desires of reason and the moral
imagination of the "better part of men," the element of the audience that is "discriminating."

On the other hand, no poem is "excellent" unless it provides
"delight." And unquestionably the "irregular" *Furioso* gives
infinitely more pleasure "to men of our time" than something like
the *Italia liberata* or even the *Iliad* or *Odyssey*. But Tasso insists
that this is the result of factors that are "accidental to the issue of
multiplicity or unity of plot." It is not the multiple plot of the

Furioso, but "that charm in imaginative inventions that makes the romances so pleasing." In order to give pleasure to everyone, to "common people" and to "the discriminating," and to appeal to those aspects of each individual which are "common" or "discriminating," the poet need not look to "multiplicity of plot," but rather to the attractive subjects of the *Furioso.* Here also lies the source of the other large category of pleasurable experience in epic poetry, variety.

For a heroic poem to be successful now, it must provide variety. Tasso reflects an acute awareness of the demands of contemporary sensibility. Here, as in other parts of the *Discorsi,* he is discriminating and sophisticated in his use of the classical culture which he sees as the source of the genuine heroic tradition. Even great examples of unified epics like the *Iliad* or *Aeneid,* let alone dubious ones like Trissino's, cannot move or delight a contemporary audience as profoundly as the *Furioso.* He hints that this is a symptom of his audience's more jaded sensibility, that there has been a decline from the general grandeur of the culture that produced the ancient poems (p. 35). The sense that the "delicate taste" of weak, if not perverse, readers requires additions to plain truths reappears in his defense of the ornaments *(fregi)* with which his pages are adorned in the invocation to the *Gerusalemme.* And in the poem, the elements identified here as sources of delight and variety, the "loves, knightly adventures and enchantments," that attractive subject matter from the romance tradition, acquire new and more complex moral and psychological connotations, producing much of the tragic drama characteristic of the *Liberata.*

But Tasso is obviously not defending the use of this subject matter or the idea of variety simply as necessary evils. To create a heroic poem with the coherence and clearly defined order of a classical epic by limiting it to a single action, while incorporating a vast array of the most attractive episodes, characters, and effects from the Italian romances, becomes the supreme achievement of a great artificer.

> Such variety will be more praiseworthy, the more difficult it is to achieve. For it is very easy and requires little effort to give truth to a great variety of accidents in many, separate actions, but to create that same variety in a single action, *hoc opus, hic labor est.* (P. 36)

In keeping with the general tone of professionalism in the *Discorsi,* he envisions this grand reconciliation of two apparently opposing strands in the tradition as a virtuoso's prize, the proof of the "skill [*arte*] and genius [*ingegno*] of the poet." Rather than defending further the idea that epic and romance are one genre, he assumes the genre "heroic poems," and describes its imagined epitome.

> The form and plot must be one, as in every other poem so in poems that deal with the arms and loves of heroes and knights-errant and are in common called by the name heroic poems. (P. 36)

Because the combination of these two versions of the heroic tradition has important consequences for the *Gerusalemme liberata*, we must note that the symmetrical syntax of the sentence suggests a significant pairing of character and episode, "arms" with "heroes" and "loves" with "knights-errant." While asserting that both kinds of heroic action belong to the epic, Tasso nevertheless maintains the distinction between them. Traditionally "heroes" and "knights-errant" do differ in behavior, motivation, and in the heroic code they embody. By naming them together and yet continuing to allow for essential distinctions between them Tasso's theoretical position opens up the possibility of a new meaning for "heroic" in Italian literature.

Within the framework of the *Discorsi*, the idea of variety ordered within a unified action leads to Tasso's most expansive and powerful vision of the poet's achievement. In expounding the need for variety in a poem aimed at a modern audience, he compares the full, well-ordered poem to "this wonderful realm of God, called the world" and the "excellent poet" to "the supreme Artificer." As I have argued, the effect of this passage is the creation of a particularly rich analogy between the inclusive order of God's work (the world) and the poet's (the epic poem). "Variety" as opposed to "multiplicity of plot" clearly offers the key to a range as inclusive as the poet's genius can successfully shape into a coherent structure. The sheer weight and energy of the language Tasso uses to express the idea demonstrate his great attraction to such an image of his poem and to those elements in experience and literature that he sees as the source for such richness. As a theoretician of the genre, he succeeds in creating an equally ordered but inclusive vision of the ideal poem, inclusive in its reconciliation of opposing literary and moral traditions, eclectic in the critical traditions on which he bases himself, and even in the kinds of reasoning he uses to argue his points.

His discussion, in the third discourse, of the proper language for epic provides a further analogy. He maintains a perfectly clear idea of the predominant qualities in a heroic style—"magnificence," "the sublime." The epic poet speaks

> like one whom we believe to be full of the deity and lifted above himself by divine furor, much above common usage, so that he seems to think and speak almost with another mind and another tongue. (P. 42)

The quite conventional reference to the poet's "divine furor" accords completely with Tasso's elevated vision of the heroic poem throughout the *Discorsi*. But this part of the treatise is, if anything, the most technical and professional of all. It formulates in detail how to create that special, extraordinary language of epic poetry which can be called "magnificent."

Characteristically, Tasso conceives of magnificence as arising from a combination and modification of two opposing kinds of language, the "simple gravity" *(semplice gravità)* appropriate to tragedy and the "intricate loveliness" *(fiorita vaghezza)* of lyric. At times, in his view, the epic poet would approach one or the other pole depending on the subject matter. Emotional scenes or direct dialogue require a language closer to the simple purity and gravity of tragedy. But when the poet speaks in his own persona, or in the intervals of repose and contemplation that can occur even in epic, he does so in a more ornamented, complex style, more like lyric.

In the discussion of language, as in considerations of subject matter and structure, Tasso writes with a sense of the grandeur and seriousness of epic. Grandeur, however, means inclusiveness, scope, as well as elevation and sustained dignity. Thus, he is able to accommodate in the highest and noblest form romantic elements of plot and character, and lyric complexity in language.

The *Discorsi*, written "for self-mastery," create the expectation, above all, that the poem will include the richness and wonder of romance shaped by laws as eternal as those of reason and nature, laws whose literary embodiments are the heroic poems of classical antiquity. That this expectation for epic also carries, in the traditions on which it is based, and in its language, a moral and religious orientation, remains implicit in the *Discorsi*. But such implications in the choice of subject matter, structure, and style become manifest as the poem unfolds, and as the essentially conflicting moral and psychological connotations of Tasso's choices reveal themselves.

3

La Gerusalemme liberata:
The Revaluation of the Classical Heroic

THE *Gerusalemme liberata* opens on a high Virgilian note that
asserts its place in the tradition of narrative poetry celebrating a
"glorious enterprise." In contrast to the Ariostan array of "*donne*
[ladies], *cavalier* [knights], *amori* [loves], *arme* [arms], *cortesie*
[courtesies], *audaci imprese* [bold deeds]" (I, i),[1] Tasso's invocation claims as the poem's subject the classically restrained "arme
pietose e'l capitano" (pious arms and the captain). His first stanza,
with a movement parallel to the opening of the *Aeneid*, seems to
declare the classical allegiance of this poem. It will be a Christian
Iliad or *Aeneid:* "arme *pietose*," "il capitano/ che'l gran sepolcro
liberò *di Cristo*" (the captain who liberated Christ's great tomb) (I,
1).

But Tasso shapes this very invocation, its language resonant
with classical echoes, in *ottava rima*.[2] This immediately complicates our sense of literary tradition and associations from the past.
The lines may offer a parallel to Virgil's opening statement of
subject, but their poetic shape, the pattern of rhyme and meter,
takes the traditional form of chivalric romance, not an Italian version of Latin hexameters. In the context of this invocation's intense
classical echoes, the stanza embodies Tasso's response to the modernist who would see ottava rima and its traditional subjects as the
only natural vein of narrative poetry for the Italian language. Here
in the traditional Italian verse form is an equivalent to genuine epic
in the high classical manner. The intimacy of the connection be-

tween a statement and its verse form becomes a metaphor for the union of epic and romance in the poem as a whole.

We can appropriately discern such literary self-consciousness here, because the poet himself speaks to the complications of tradition involved in his enterprise. As though responding directly to the classical parallels of the opening stanza, he immediately appeals to a muse (just as Virgil does), but explicitly not the muse invoked by Homer or Virgil: "O Musa, tu che di caduchi allori/ Non circondi la fronte in Elicona (O Muse, you who do not garland your brow with fallen laurels in Helicon) (I, 2). The poet, in propria persona, deliberately points up the contrast between classical and Christian epic. At the same time he infuses his language with all the power and authority derived from his direct evocation of the Greek and Latin models for his Italian.

The classical muse, the poetry inspired by the powers of Parnassus, represent not only ancient culture, but poetry itself seen as pleasure and easy delight. The poet registers his awareness of the attractions felt by "il mondo" (the world, his audience of average men) for the "dolcezze" (sweets) provided by "il lusinghier Parnaso" (alluring Parnassus). This world is full of those who are "schivi" (reluctant) in the face of truth, like sick children in need of medicine to give them life. Along with this sense of a fallen world, he imparts a highly critical attitude toward the "dolcezze," the "molli versi" (soft verses), in which the truth must be hidden. At this point he employs the old image of "soavi licor" (sweet syrups) used to disguise the "amari" (bitter [medicine]) needed by the "ingannato" (deceived), who still receives "vita" (life) out of such deception. These aspects of poetry he calls "fregi" (ornaments), and apologizes because he must "adorn" his verse with "altri diletti che de' tuoi" (other delights than yours [the Christian Muse's], I, 2).

This language directly reflects Christian-Platonic attacks on the falsity of poetry, particularly poetry modeled on the classics. It complicates the sense of this poem's positive relation to classical culture, apparent in the opening stanza. As the poem unfolds, however, the "dolcezze" with which plain truth is adorned also come to be associated with the "romantic" elements of the poem, evoked here by the verse form.

Nevertheless, the poet's voice does create a highly ambivalent relationship between this epic and its classical models. By opening the poem as he does, Tasso immediately sets up positive associations with ancient epic. He achieves grandeur and seriousness of tone, in large measure, through the resonances from Greek and Latin in his language. But he devalues the culture from which that greatness arose as the "soavi licor" needed to lure the childish irrationality of fallen man, who must receive his "life" from "deceit." And yet this very image, through which he finds poetic expression for his critical attitude toward classical culture, is itself modeled on Lucretius.[3] Tasso founds his poem on the paradoxical devaluation of a classical world which nevertheless provides his only real examples of epic.

We must, therefore, distinguish Tasso's classical manner—the basic structure derived from ancient epic, the echoes of language and imagery, the Latinization of vocabulary to achieve a "classical" magnificence—from the imitation of classical poetry in theme and values. The worth of epic as a poetic enterprise derives ultimately from ancient precedent and the value placed on it by Tasso's culture. The sense of high seriousness pervading the poem begins from the cultural expectations of the form created by ancient tradition. And Tasso constantly shapes his language to achieve effects that resemble ancient grandeur, as in his opening stanza. But he also immediately uses direct classical allusions ("allori . . . in Elicona," "il lusinghier Parnaso") critically, as referents for negative values that become temptations for the sensibilities of fallen men.

The direct imitation of classical culture tends to occur in this ambivalent or negative context. Classical allusions, images derived from Graeco-Roman mythology, and overt uses of ancient literature or history are almost exclusively confined to situations that involve pagan characters or demons. Tasso constantly associates such imagery with Armida, for instance. She is more beautiful than Venus (IV, 29); she accomplishes with her wiles more than Circe or Medea, and talks in the voice of a Siren (IV, 86). In her deceptive appeal to the Christian warriors, she calls on "Jove" as the God shared by all (IV, 42). When the warriors do succumb to her wiles and fall prey to love, they are compared to "fierce Achilles" and to "Hercules and Theseus" (IV, 96). At other moments in the poem, Tasso compares her to Proteus (VI, 63), to Narcissus at the fountain (XIV, 66), to Cleopatra deserting Antony in battle (XX, 118).

Not only does he identify Armida, the reincarnation of Circe, with the classical world, but whenever he uses a directly classical image, it refers to a character or situation defined as evil in the poem. The description of Armida's garden abounds with allusions to ancient mythology, and achieves much of its appeal by evoking the *"locus amoenus"* and "golden age" motifs as they appear in ancient literature.[4] The poet summons such language at various moments for other pagan characters, like Argante, Solimano, or Clorinda. He compares Argante in VI, 23 to Enceladus, Solimano in IX, 3 to the giants who rebelled against Jove, and gives Clorinda in XI, 28 the expected analogy to Diana. Classical references define even minor pagan characters. The King of Egypt, described on his throne in XVII, is a "thundering Jove" as conceived by Apelles or Phidias, and he commands his generals in an echo of Caesar, "Va', vedi e vinci" (Go, see and conquer, XVII, 38). The magician, Ismeno, with his helpers on the walls of Jerusalem resembles "Charon or Pluto between two Furies" (XVIII, 87). The demons themselves follow a Satan with the classical name of *Plutone* (Pluto). They are particularized as the monsters known from Graeco-Roman mythology, "Harpies, Centaurs, Sphinxes and pale Gorgons . . . gaping Scyllas . . . Hydras and Pythons . . . Chimeras . . . horrifying Polyphemuses and Geryons" (IV, 5), as though all the hellish creatures of antiquity had gathered for the torment of the Crusaders.

Rarely, on the other hand, does Tasso use overtly classical language about the Christian warriors. Raimondo, when he takes on the challenge of single combat against Argante in VII, is told that he resembles Mars in honor, skill, and discipline (VII, 68). The poet again invokes Mars to describe a Christian's superiority in war when Rinaldo arms himself in V, 44. He once compares Gildippe to an Amazon, and Tancredi battling Argante to Hercules overcoming the giant. This is the extent of the direct classical allusions used positively to characterize Christians. And in some of these examples (for instance, the lines about Raimondo), the classical reference works more as a figure of speech than as an actual image, meant to call up the referent in classical literature.

This limited, purely rhetorical use of classical allusion applies also to a few "neutral" instances, such as VI, 55, where "l'incerto Marte" (uncertain Mars) appears as a figure for the varying fortunes of war, or the line describing the final battle in XX, "Sta dubbia in mezzo la Fortuna e Marte" (It remains doubtful between Fortune and Mars, XX, 72). Tasso's defense of this particular line in a letter to Scipione Gonzaga reveals how self-consciously he employed such allusions:

It might seem to someone that I introduce pagan gods. If that is so, let

us eliminate these and all other similar expressions. But I continue to
believe that these words have been so molded by usage [*ammollite*, lit.
softened], that now they signify and are understood by men to signify
only that the outcome of the war was doubtful because the valor of the
soldiers was equally balanced. I think these expressions should be
classified under that figure of speech (I don't know what it's called) in
which the name of the deity is used instead of the thing he represents.
There are some similar comparisons in the poem . . . to Jove or Brontes
for example. . . . Comparisons (I speak of poetic ones) are not made
solely to declare, but often simply for ornament; therefore they can be
drawn not only from true and natural things . . . but also from famous
things.[5]

Here, he calls on the cultural prevalence of pagan references to
defend them as simply appropriate figures of speech. He is exploit-
ing one of many ways of talking about war available in the language because of historical and literary tradition. Clearly,
however, he feels that references to "pagan gods" require defense,
and that one could eliminate this kind of language altogether. Classical allusions, once a hallmark of any Italian literature with claims
to seriousness or lasting value, are now suspect and could be seen
as defects in style. In the poem a more decisive moral evaluation
arises from the fact that classical references figure in the representation of the evil forces, the obstacles to the conquest of
Jerusalem and to the Crusaders' fulfillment of their vows. Though
these figures of speech are often of the most commonplace and
expected sorts, Tasso confines them to pagan contexts.

The mere use of obviously classical images, however, cannot
account for this poem's complex relationship to ancient literature.
From the opening lines it asserts its place in the tradition of epic
defined primarily by the Greek and Roman examples. The very
idea of an epic poem was inevitably embedded in associations with
those poems that all readers in Renaissance Europe knew as the
best examples of the form. In the language that claims a place in the
continuing European epos, Tasso also associates his poem with the
heroic values, the vision of the heroic life incarnated in such poems
as the *Iliad* or *Aeneid*. Though in his theoretical writing on epic, he
successfully presents the issues as technical ones, he is nevertheless
talking about "the *heroic* poem". In supporting the relevance of
ancient models, he must come to terms with what is meant by
heroic in those poems. The *Discorsi* use the term *epic (epopeia)*
synonymously with *heroic poem (poema eroico)*. The creation of a
Christian epic therefore implies some incorporation of the themes,

the style of life, or the values of ancient epic, as well as its structure and diction. Particularly when the poet implies, as Tasso does in the *Discorsi*, a sense of moral, as well as aesthetic, allegiance to classical epic, he invites the reader to consider the fate of classical heroic values in his poem.

Critics have conventionally represented the poem in parallel dichotomies: the heroic vs. the romantic, or military as opposed to emotional (amorous) subject matter. This method of analysis has tended to limit the "heroic" to "military action." Giovanni Getto, for instance, in an essay entitled "Goffredo e il tema epico-religioso," like Tasso makes the terms *epico* and *eroico* synonymous. Because of the incidents he chooses to discuss under this title, Getto expresses quite rigorously the sense that the epic or heroic element of the poem relates only to the Crusade literally construed as a military action. He tells us, for instance, that Rinaldo achieves "heroic stature" only in the cantos where he is actually involved in a literal battle.[6] Other major critics, like De Sanctis, Croce, or Donadoni, use the terms *epic* and *heroic* similarly to define separate elements in the poem.[7]

Many critics writing in English have continued to assume a "heroic" structural element in the poem that should be distinguished from elements of "romance."[8] C. P. Brand, for instance, subsumes under the concept "heroic ideal" or the "Classical," battles, duels, and the military aspect in general, the "Christian supernatural," and the historical basis of the poem. He contrasts all this to the "chivalrous romance," which Tasso "includes." "The heroic ideal is *adulterated* [my italics] therefore with the charms of the romances—notably the loves and enchantments—and Tasso admits his compromise from the beginning." According to Brand, Tasso compromises ". . . between the heroic, serious, didactic elements on the one hand and the fanciful and romantic on the other . . ." (p. 80).

But to perceive the "heroic" as limited to the military is to deform the poem. Tasso marshals his imaginative resources in the *Gerusalemme liberata* to represent a larger understanding of the heroic centered on the inner life. As one stage in such a reevaluation he does make use of a classical ideal of heroism, but as only one element in the sense of the heroic that emerges from the poem as a whole.

Tasso embodies this classical heroic ideal most fully in those heroes who live according to a code of integrity and honor as supremely effective warriors. Like the Homeric heroes, these

characters perform brilliantly in battle, facing death without illusions, for the sake of glory. Tasso also suggests in such masterful
characters an awareness of fate and "a recognition of the tragic
mystery of all heroic violence."[9]

Sometimes when Tasso speaks the language of this heroic vision,
its negative contexts ensure a critical tone to the expression of
ancient epic values. A clearly classical heroic language occurs, for
instance, early in the poem, in the council of demons (Canto IV).
This recalls the conventional epic episodes of councils of the gods
in various ancient epics. By also sounding strong echoes of Dante's
language in *Inferno* for the grotesque horror of these creatures of
evil,[10] Tasso presents the devils (especially Plutone) as debased
versions of classical heroes. Out of the overwhelming sounds and
sights of a Dantean hell, the voice of Plutone calling on the "Tartarei numi" (Tartarean gods, IV, 9) resounds with the injured dignity of defeated grandeur. He tells his cohorts they are "più degni"
(more worthy) to dwell above the sun and sees their present horrors as brought on them by "il gran caso" (great chance). He recalls
"l'alta impresa nostra" (our high enterprise) when they aspired to
"il primo onor" (the first honor). And he claims for himself and
the other demons the bitterness of the vanquished, as he counts up
the indignities suffered in defeat. The final exhortation to action in
the Crusade on the pagan side resonates with the language of ancient heroism:

> Ah! non fia ver; ché non sono anco estinti
> Gli spirti in voi di quel valor primiero,
> Quando di ferro e d'alte fiamme cinti
> Pugnammo già contra il celeste impero.
> Fummo, io no'l nego, in quel conflitto vinti:
> Pur non mancò virtute al gran pensiero.
> Diede che che si fosse a lui vittoria:
> Rimase a noi d'invitto ardir la gloria.
>
> (IV, 15)

Ah let it not be true; for not yet extinct in you are the spirits of that
first valor, when, girded with leaping flames and iron we fought
against the heavenly empire. I cannot deny that we were conquered in
that conflict; but there still was greatness in the great idea. The powers
that be gave the victory to him. To us remained the glory of unconquered daring.

In Plutone Tasso creates a spirit of ancient self-glorification and
concern for honor in victory or revenge. But he constantly juxta-

poses the language infused with that spirit to the moral evaluation of the Christian view. These are "l'alme a Dio rubelle" (the souls rebellious to God, IV, 18). Plutone, speaking in grand tones to his "Tartarei numi," is "il gran nemico de l'umane genti" (the great enemy of humankind, IV, 1), and the "numi" he addresses are described with all the bestial, fearsome imagery to be derived from Dante. The associations from the *Commedia* combined with the language of ancient grandeur serve to debase that classical rhetoric. The talk of glory, of high enterprise, of fidelity to a noble self-conception even in defeat here becomes vainglory, a devalued heroism. This moral effect emerges even more clearly when Plutone outlines his plan for harassing the Christians. For the offensive to be mounted by these "heroes" will consist of seduction and deceit, an effort to make the Crusaders (like the demons themselves) into a "stuol ribellante e'n sé diviso" (rebellious mob, divided against itself, IV, 17) by allying with the base passions within them. The grand language of the demons rings hollow, through its unequivocal juxtaposition with the moral language that reveals their evil.

But Tasso also creates classical heroes among the pagan warriors, embodying values not so easily overthrown. He compares Argante and Solimano, Clorinda and the minor pagan warriors, to the Titans, challenging Jove and demanding superhuman force to be defeated. Tasso asks us to understand the pagans as warriors living by the ancient heroic code from our first view of Argante and Alete when they go as ambassadors to the Christian camp.[11] Alete bases his presentation of their mission on the assumptions of that code. In his address to Goffredo, Alete stresses the theme of "honor," renown gained through conquest and military prowess. He adopts the formal rhetoric of address familiar from similar speeches in classical epic (e.g., the elaborate symmetry of the opening in II, 62, "O degno sol cui d'ubidire or degni," O you who are the only worthy one [this assembly of heroes] now deigns to obey). His language about Goffredo and the other Crusaders implies their identification with traditional warriors: they are "famosi eroi" (famous heroes); Goffredo's name "non rimane tra i segni/ D'Alcide" (goes beyond the pillars of Hercules [Alcides]) and all Egypt knows of his "valor." His proposal to Goffredo assumes that the two opposing armies have not been inevitably forced into combat because they represent good battling evil. Instead he insinuates that they share an ambition for glory and conquest and the knowledge of *Realpolitik* necessary to achieve them.

According to Alete, the King of Egypt is attracted to Goffredo because "ama il valore" (he loves valor, II, 63) and for this reason would join with him in achieving "L'amicizia e la pace" (friendship and peace, II, 64). He feels that they can be brought together, despite the difference in faith, because of their common respect for "virtù": "E'l mezzo, onde l'un resti a l'altro avvinto, / Sia la virtù s'esser non può la fede" (And let the means by which one remains bound to the other be heroic virtue, if it cannot be faith, II, 64). He joins this praise of "virtù" to rather Machiavellian talk about sharing the power in Asia, creating an image of the Crusade as a traditional war of conquest, undertaken for "gloria" (glory) and "imperio" (empire, II, 67). According to him, they all risk losing "onor" in case of failure.

Tasso immediately subverts such an interpretation of the Crusade, insisting that we must read this war as religious quest. He has already characterized Alete, the voice of the morally meaningless "reading" of the Crusade, as a deceiver and flatterer. The response of the Christians further rejects this view of their war. Goffredo speaks directly to the assumptions behind Alete's oratory by asserting a completely different set of motives for their warfare. They are not interested, he says, in "onor mondano e vita e regno" (earthly honor, life, and rule, II, 82), but have exercised all their prowess solely to open the way to "quelle sacre e venerabil mura / Per acquistar appo Dio grazia e merto" (those sacred and venerable walls in order to acquire grace and merit with God, II, 82). In fact, he sees "ambizïosi avari affetti" (greedy, ambitious passions, II, 83), as a poison which he must pray God to remove from his warriors, if any of them do respond to the call of "onor." He calls the love of glory "venen dolce che piacendo ancida" (a sweet poison that kills in pleasing, II, 83), and answers the calculations and maneuvering of *Realpolitik* by a deliberately simple assertion of faith. Goffredo refuses even to speak in the terms Alete presents. The pagan's view of the nature of the war is classed with the temptations of Plutone and his minions.

Here a narrative event devalues ancient conventions about the goals of war, and substitutes a Christian moral definition of the battle. As in the history of Western epic, the narrative moves from a conception of conflict involving morally equal human and historical differences to the idea that conflict is caused by the inevitable clash of good and evil.

Though these early episodes call for a negative response to the ancient view of heroism, Tasso presents other pagan characters in a more complex and sympathetic version of the classical vision of a great man. Rather than devil worshipers, the pagans eventually attain the dignity of doomed defenders of a cause, fighting and dying for a limited but still noble ethic. Argante, for instance, the other ambassador to the Christian camp, immediately displays the character, not of a deceiver and flatterer, but of one who lives true to his own faith, "che ripone / Ne la spada sua legge e sua razione" (who places in his sword his law and reason, II, 59).[12] Argante's part in the embassy dramatizes his constant ferocity and open battle hunger. From him comes a challenge to "guerra Mortal" (war to the death), which the poet directly associates with classical images of war and fury:

> . . .—A guerra mortal, disse, vi sfido;—
> E'l disse in atto sì feroce ed empio,
> Che parve aprir di Giano il chiuso tempio.
>
> Parve, ch'aprendo il seno, indi traesse
> Il furor pazzo e la discordia fèra;
> E che, ne gli occhi orribili gli ardesse
> La gran face d'Aletto e di Megera.
>
> (II, 90–91)

He spoke: "I challenge you to war to the death";—And he spoke in such a fierce and pitiless manner that the closed temple of Janus seemed to open.

He looked like one who, opening his breast, drew forth mad fury and savage discord; in his terrible eyes burned the great torch of Allecto and Megara.[13]

As though responding to the ancient image of warfare presented in this embassy, Goffredo honors them with gifts of helmet and sword, which the narrator describes in a convention taken straight from Homer.

But Tasso does not limit the classical nature of the pagans' ethic to a few episodes based on epic convention. Whenever the poet speaks from their point of view, he constructs a classical world. In the opening of Canto XII, for instance, a debate with Argante marks the prelude to Clorinda's death. The warrior maiden tries to persuade him that he must not join her in burning the Christians' tower, because he is an essential defender whose death would mean disaster to the city. Argante disdains this kind of argument, seeing it as a mere excuse to keep him from danger and glory:

> No no; se fui ne l'arme a te consorte
> Esser vo' ne la gloria e ne la morte.

> Ho core anch'io, che morte sprezza, e crede
> Che ben si cambi con l'onor la vita.
>
> (XII, 7, 8)

No, no—if I have been your companion in arms, I want to be so also in glory and death.

I, too, have a heart that disdains death and believes that one does well to exchange life for honor.

To the titanic hero no general cause requires him to refrain from acting on his sense of honor and personal integrity.

This provides an exact contrast to the action of Goffredo in Canto VII, when no one in the Christian camp appeared to answer Argante's challenge to single combat. Goffredo offers to take up the challenge to preserve the honor of the Crusaders:

> . . .—Ah! ben sarei di vita indegno,
> Se la vita negassi o porre in forse,
> Lasciando ch'un pagan così vilmente
> Calpestasse l'onor di nostra gente.
>
> (VII, 60)

Ah! I would indeed be unworthy of life if I failed to risk my life, letting a pagan so vilely trample the honor of our people.

But he is restrained by the same argument that fails to move Argante for an instant. The experienced Raimondo reminds him that "Duce sei tu, non semplice guerriero;/ Publico fôra, e non privato il lutto" (You are the leader, not a simple warrior; the fight would be a public, not a private matter, VII, 62). Goffredo agrees to forgo the exercise of his personal valor for the sake of the cause.

Later in Canto XII, Clorinda chooses to disregard the revelation of her Christian infancy, remaining unmoved by the issue of abstract "truth" and "falsehood" in her religion. Her old servant ends the recital of Clorinda's early history by warning her of portents and dreams, and suggests that Clorinda may be defying heaven by fighting against the true faith. Clorinda is momentarily troubled, but immediately falls back on the typical pagan ethic:

> Quella fé seguirò che vera or parmi,
> Che tu co'l latte già de la nutrice

Sugger mi fêsti, e che vuoi dubbia or farmi:
Né per temenza lascierò, né lice
A magnanimo cor, l'impresa e l'armi;
Non se la morte nel più fier sembiante
Che sgomenti i mortali avessi inante.

(XII, 41)

I will follow that faith that seems true to me now, that faith that you
made me suck in with my nurse's milk and that you now want me to
doubt: nor will I leave this enterprise and my arms through fear, nor
would it be permitted to a great and noble heart, not even if death were
before me in the fiercest guise with which it terrifies mortals.

The truth by which she can live depends solely on personal integrity, on what has been given her to do, not on an abstract, metaphysical conviction. Despite the matter for doubt given by her servant, she insists on remaining true to her self-image and to the values of the "magnanimo cor." And this leads her to her death. Argante expresses the tragic sense of both pagans when he declares that "Ella morì di fatal morte" (she died a death decreed by fate) and vows revenge. She died a death decreed by fate, true to her sense of honor and personal valor. This constitutes worth and greatness to the pagan characters.

Even the minor characters, the Egyptian warriors who fight the final battle under the walls of Jerusalem, end their lives in self-conscious adherence to this ideal of heroic action. Emireno rallies his fleeing soldiers by calling on their sense of honor "Combatta qui chi di campar desìa:/ La via d'onor de la salute è via" (He who wants to save himself must fight here: the path of honor is the path to salvation, XX, 110). The warrior Tisaferno does "meraviglie" solely for the sake of "honor in the praises of men" with full consciousness of his impending doom:

Poi ch'a le mete de l'onor eterno
La vita breve prolungò co' fatti,
Quasi di viver più poco gli caglia,
Cerca il rischio maggior de la battaglia.

(XX, 112)

Then, he prolonged his brief life with great deeds done for the sake of
eternal honor. He seeks out the greatest danger in the battle, as if
longer life matters little to him.

The final stages of the battle reveal the pagans fighting only for their own integrity, in full awareness of the futility of their cause. In death they demonstrate the ethic by which they have been living.

Solimano, the most self-conscious of the pagan heroes, explicitly invokes this code of values. At the end of the horrifying battle in Canto IX, when Christian forces aided by direct intervention from heaven drive back the pagans at great cost to both sides, Solimano reluctantly gives up the fight. In response to the necessity for retreat he contemplates suicide. He decides to let fate conquer only to play the part of eternal defiance and never-wearying battle, whether or not his cause succeeds or he even survives:

> Non cedo io, no; fia con memoria eterna
> De le mie offese eterno anco il mio sdegno.
> Risorgerò nemico ognor più crudo,
> Cenere anco sepolto e spirto ignudo.
>
> (IX, 99)

I do not yield, no; with the eternal memory of my wrongs let my defiance also be eternal. I will arise again, an enemy always more savage, even when a corpse or disembodied spirit.

This is the authentic voice of the titanic hero, unadulterated by moral ambiguities. The powerful and simple declaration ("non cedo io, no") followed by the symmetry of the hortative clause resonates with both the syntax and vocabulary of ancient heroism.

Solimano speaks this language throughout the poem. In the next canto, for instance, when he is taken up by Ismeno, he responds to the magician's challenge by asserting his own desire for the path of greatest danger:

> Padre, risponde, io già pronto e veloce
> Sono a seguirti; ove tu vuoi mi gira.
> A me sempre miglior parrà il consiglio
> Ove ha più di fatica e di periglio.
>
> (X, 13)

He answers, Father, I am ready and eager to follow you; lead me where you will. To me the best counsel will always be that which has most effort and danger.

A few stanzas later he compares his own integrity to the immutable laws of nature:

> . . . Girisi pur Fortuna
> O buona o rea, come è là su prescritto;
> Ché non ha sovra me ragione alcuna,
> E non mi vedrà mai, se non invitto.
> Prima dal corso distornar la luna
> E le stelle potrà, che dal diritto
> Torcere un sol mio passo. . . .
>
> (X, 24)

Let Fortune turn for good or evil, as it is determined above; for she has no law over me and will never see me, unless unconquered. The moon and stars could wander from their orbits sooner than I could turn one step away from the right.

His vaguely classical terms, "Fortuna," "là su prescritto," "il diritto," express an attitude familiar from the heroic rhetoric of ancient literature.

He regards himself rightly as one of the grand forces aiding the pagan cause. When he suddenly appears in the midst of the king's council in Jerusalem (X, 14–56) he is not merely present, but shines forth, a luminous power suddenly infusing his allies with strength. His presence and solidity alone sway the king to confidence and resolution.

This "marvelous" appearance of Solimano insures that the pagans remain constant to the view also expressed in this episode by Argante. That "undaunted, fierce warrior" speaks, as always, in the voice of eternal defiance and loyalty to the ethic of personal honor. He urges:

> . . . sia la speme in noi sol posta:
> E s'egli è ver che nulla a virtù nòce,
> Di questa armiamci: a lei chiediamo aita;
> Né più ch'ella si vaglia, amiam la vita.
>
> (X, 37)

Let our hope be placed in ourselves alone. If it is true that nothing can harm virtue, let us arm ourselves with it and seek our aid from it. And let us not love life more than it is worth.

The narrator adds to the nobility of this tone by contrasting it to the speech of Orcano urging surrender. Orcano, he suggests, has allowed time to conquer. Though he used to be "d'alta nobiltà famosa/ . . . Ma or . . . era invilito/ Ne gli affetti di padre e di marito" (famous for his nobility, but now he was made cowardly by the feelings of a father and husband, X, 39). Tasso in this episode clearly considers Argante's to be the voice of greatness when he calls for: "In alcuni di noi spirto più invitto, / Ch'egualmente apprestato ad ogni sorte / Si prometta vittoria, e sprezzi morte" (a more indomitable spirit in some of us, a spirit ready for any fate, a spirit that will promise victory and disdain death, X, 38).

The language defining these two titanic figures, Argante and Solimano, strongly suggests the classical past. Their heroism depends on an ethic whose authority derives from ancient literature and philosophy. They represent what is admirable among the pagans. And Tasso does express admiration, "meraviglia," in moving his audience to feel pity and wonder at their fate. These two figures stride through the landscape of the poem, distinct, isolated individuals, powerful because they fulfill the expectations created by a classical heroic language.

We experience, nonetheless, the force of great men in defeat, doomed heroes. Their fate determines the boundaries of a classical heroic vision in Tasso's poem. He incorporates the poetry of ancient heroism into his epic as tragedy subsumed within the larger movement toward salvation. These two characters are the best examples in the poem of Tasso's "poesia titanica" (titanic poetry), "poesia dei grandi sconfitti" (poetry of grand defeats), in Donadoni's phrase.[14] They move us as characters in ancient tragedy do, grand, isolated figures, larger than life. Because they live according to an admirable sense of personal integrity they seem worthy of being victorious. But they are doomed because they stand against an immutable Fate.

They represent, however, two distinct versions of tragic characterization.[15] Argante incarnates the most elemental aggression. He isolates himself from any human relationship or limit in order to follow freely the impulse to violent action. Solimano, like Aeneas, has a past, and therefore a reason for fighting that is comprehensible in human terms. His defiance arises from an intense need for revenge rather than from pure violent force. Rather than refusing human relationships or limits, he endures the solitude of the exile and leader. His royal status and the ties binding his action to a past give plausibility to his concern for history. He consciously acts out not only his individual fate but his part in the fate of nations, as in Canto X, when he asks Ismeno, during their magic journey into Jerusalem, to tell him about the fate of "Asia" as a whole. He also feels the anguish of comrades' death (e.g., the Lesbino episode in IX) and his cause's defeat, unlike Argante, who is generally unmoved by death and fights only for his own sense of self.

In the last act of Solimano's tragedy, Tasso develops this character's potentiality for a heroism of the interior life. Several times at the end of the battle Solimano reveals his sense that royalty, heroism, or grandeur derive from inner attitudes. When the pagan king, Aladino, declares "Noi fummo . . . non vivo più, né regno" (We have been. I no longer live nor reign, XIX, 40), Solimano immediately recalls him to "la tua virtute" (your virtue), for "Tolgaci i regni pur sorte nemica;/ Ché'l regal pregio è nostro, e'n noi dimora" (Hostile fate can take away only realms from us, but the prize of royalty is ours and dwells within us, XIX, 41). In his final exhortation to the soldiers he pleads eloquently that they concentrate only on the inner reality of their own valor, not on the material conquest of walls and streets by their enemies. Solimano achieves a final tragic consciousness just before going to his death, a heightening of this strain in his character. Tasso lifts his sense of history and individual suffering, and his recognition of the grandeur always possible within, to a plane of religious understanding of the human condition. When he acts, he does so in full awareness of his own tragic fate and the tragedy of humanity in general.

> Salse in cima a la torre ad un balcone,
> E mirò, ben che lunge, il fèr Soldano:
> Mirò, quasi in teatro od in agone,
> L'aspra tragedia de lo stato umano,
> I vari assalti, e il fèro orror di morte,
> E i gran giochi del caso e de la sorte.
>
> Stette attonito alquanto e stupefatto
> A quelle prime viste; e poi s'accese,
> E desïò trovarsi anch'egli in atto
> Nel periglioso campo a l'alte imprese:

(XX, 73–74)

The fierce Sultan mounted to the top of the tower to a balcony and looked, though it was far away.

He looked, as in a theater or an arena, on the harsh tragedy of the human condition, the varying combats, and savage terror of death, and the great plays of chance and fate.

He stood somewhat amazed, stupefied at these sights and then he kindled, and wanted to be himself in action in the perilous field of high deeds.

Argante at the end also achieves a moment of awareness, fighting on with a tragic consciousness of a doom that he will deliberately ignore for the sake of his own greatness in action. He pauses for a brief moment, as though lifted from his customary impetuosity to a state of suspension out of himself. He responds seriously to Tancredi's taunt of cowardice with his own heightened sense of the larger fate in which he is involved:

> Penso, risponde, a la città del regno
> Di Giudea antichissima regina,
> Che vinta or cade; e indarno esser sostegno
> Io procurai de la fatal rüina:
> E ch'è poca vendetta al mio disdegno
> Il capo tuo, che'l Cielo or mi destina.
>
> (XIX, 10)

He replies, I am thinking of the city, queen of the realm of Judea since time immemorial, now fallen conquered; and I strove in vain to be a support against its fated ruin. Small vengeance for my hatred will be your head, now destined to me by heaven.

Argante's moment of contemplation differs from Solimano's overview "come in teatro od in agone" in that it is really circumscribed within his own person.[16] He broods over the city that "*I* strove in vain to support," in this single exceptional moment of introspection before reassuming his accustomed character. Nevertheless, in these episodes expressing heightened awareness of fate, both the great pagan warriors embody a classical perception of "the tragic mystery of heroic violence." It is the supremely moving culmination to their consistent characterization as heroes of the ancient mold. And we must weigh the poet's obvious admiration for the ideal of a heroic life that they come to represent against the easy criticism of classical heroics in an episode like the council in Inferno. Tasso conceives Argante, and especially Solimano, as grand tragic figures. Particularly as they meet their fate at the hands of the great Christian warriors, they arouse emotions of pity and awe for defeated but magnificent men in the ancient tradition, without moral reflections on the good or evil of their cause.

But in the poem as a whole those who live by their ethic of personal integrity and honor are the enemy. Tasso associates the language of glory and revenge with demons, and classes the desire for "honor in the praises of men," divorced from the overriding cause, with the temptations the Crusaders must overcome to fulfill their vows. In the end, the classical idea of the heroic life is not only defeated, but morally rejected as admirable but insufficient.

To describe Argante and Solimano, Tasso consistently calls on an imagery of animals and natural forces, in addition to classical language. In a passage in which we hear Argante declaring his fatalistic determination to act according to his own honor no matter what the consequences (VI, 5), the poet surrounds him with imagery of animal fury and the blind inexorable power of natural elements. Later, when Tancredi taunts him:

> . . . il pagano, al sofferir poco uso,
> Morde le labra, e di furor si strugge:
> Risponder vuol, ma il suono esce confuso,
> Sì come strido d'animal che rugge.
>
> (VI, 38)

the pagan, little used to sufferance,
bites his lips, and is consumed with fury.
He wants to answer, but the sound emerges
unclearly, like the bellow of a roaring animal.

This echoes Tasso's earlier image for Plutone: "Ambo le labbra per furor si morse;/ E, qual tauro ferito, il suo dolore/ Versò mugghiando e sospirando fuore" (He bit both lips in fury. And like a wounded bull, his grief poured forth, bellowing and sighing, IV, 1). The analogy immediately qualifies the kind of greatness Tasso is creating for him. Epic similes for Argante also compare him to elemental powers of nature. His voice not only resembles the roar of an animal, but

> . . . come apre le nubi, ond'egli è chiuso,
> Impetüoso il fulmine, e sen fugge,
> Così pareva a forza ogni suo detto
> Tonando uscir da l'infiammato petto.
>
> (VI, 38)

as when the clouds open, and the lightning enclosed in them now hurtles forth, so it seemed that every word was forced thunderously out of his enkindled chest.

These two strands of imagery pervade the poetic configuration of this character.

Similarly, images for Solimano first compare him to the giants who rebelled against Jove (IX, 3) and to Turnus inspired by the

classical fury Allecto, but then associate him, through the battle
that follows, with the grand elements of nature (IX, 12, 49). He is
as formidable as the fearsome ocean, frequently Tasso's emblem
for the vastness and terrible mystery of the dangers surrounding
his warriors (IX, 26). The sheer weight of this imagery invests him
with overwhelming power, completely divorced from human limitations:

> Corre inanzi il Soldano, e giunge a quella
> Confusa ancora e inordinata guarda
> Rapido sì, che torbida procella
> Da' cavernosi monti esce più tarda.
> Fiume ch'arbori insieme e case svella,
> Folgore che le torri abbatta ed arda,
> Terremoto che'l mondo empia d'orrore,
> Son picciole sembianze al suo furore.
>
> (IX, 22)

The Sultan runs ahead, and reaches the still confused and disordered
guards so swiftly that a dark storm rushes down from cavernous
mountains more slowly. A river that sweeps away trees and houses
together, lightning that knocks down and burns towers, an earthquake
filling the world with terror, these are small likenesses to his fury.

Tasso also characterizes him as a mythical animal of incredible
menace. When he appears in battle in Canto IX, the poet dwells on
the horrifying device of the serpent on his helmet (IX, 25), transforming him to a sea monster, the source of dark terror. He is
often described as a voracious beast of prey, in a language equally
characteristic of Argante (e.g., X, 2).

In the ferocious nocturnal battle of Canto IX, these strands of
imagery combine to make both the great pagan warriors inhuman
beasts of prey, inexorable in their destruction as the lightning and
whirlwinds, experiencing a pleasure in slaughter that makes them
closer to the dark forces of the underworld than to shining figures
of fulfilled manhood. Even in the final great battle, when Solimano's moment of contemplation transfigures him through his
consciousness of tragic humanity, his descent into battle turns him
again into "il Turco atroce" (the atrocious Turk) wreaking destruction like the essence of all animal ferocity:

> Nessun dente giamai, nessun artiglio
> O di silvestre o d'animal pennuto
> Insanguinossi in mandra, o tra gli augelli,
> Come la spada del Soldan tra quelli

Sembra quasi famelica e vorace;
Pasce le membra quasi, e'l sangue sugge.

(XX, 78–79)

No tooth, no claw of forest or feathered beast ever was bloodied among flocks, sheep, or birds as the Sultan's sword among these fighters comes to seem like something famished and voracious. It is as though he feeds on limbs and sucks blood.

This is the battle in which Solimano meets his death. Tasso encloses his power and ferocity in almost dreamlike suspensions of action, allowing scope for the revelation of his awareness and interior resolution. Just as his eruption into battle is preceded by the contemplative overview of life "come in teatro od in agone," it is ended by a sudden clarity about his own individual fate. When he sees Rinaldo kill Adrasto with one blow, a premonition of his own death almost paralyzes this man of titanic energy. Tasso at this moment compares his state to that of someone sick or mad caught in a nightmare of overwhelming yet inescapable danger. As the poet's voice comments on the aura of inexorable fate brooding over the doomed warrior (XX, 104), it sets the scene for a drama of internal awareness of the end pitted against the determination to act according to the pagan's ethic of valor. Attacked by the "velocitade" (speed), "furore" (fury), "grandezza" (grandeur) of Rinaldo, Solimano can do almost nothing. He is oppressed by his consciousness of his own internal life, by that terrible clarity about his own fate (XX, 106). The resulting confrontation between "l'irresoluto" (the irresolute) and "il vincitore" (the conqueror), makes Solimano's death so inevitable that it happens without the necessity of describing its accomplishment. At the beginning of a line he is acting in this semiparalyzed state, and by the end of the same line he is dying, "Poco ripugna quel; pur, mentre mòre" (He hardly fights back: then while he is dying, XX, 107). In his death he remains the grand figure of action, who nevertheless reveals at crucial times the acute awareness and conscious resolution that make for tragedy.

... pur, mentre mòre,
Già non oblia la generosa usanza:
Non fugge i colpi, e gemito non spande,
Né atto fa, se non se altèro e grande.

(XX, 107)

then while dying, he never forgets his usual greatness of spirit. He neither flees the blows, nor expends a groan, nor does any deed that is not noble and grand.

This passive language, suggesting the greatness of a Stoic endurance, creates a wholly appropriate tragic denouement for this character. Through him Tasso expresses most fully in the poem the classical heroism of both the exterior sphere in martial action and the interior sphere of contemplation and tragic awareness. The death scene ends with the suggestive last image of Solimano as the classical giant Antaeus, whose final downfall signals the end of all obstacles to the Christian victory (XX, 108).

Tasso condenses in one image of Solimano in the final battle the effect of this poetry of "great defeats," of the pagan warriors as the Titans rebelling against immutable Fate:

> Grande ma breve aita apportò questi
> A' saracini impauriti e lassi.
> Grande, ma breve fulmine il diresti,
> Ch'inaspettato sopragiunga e passi,
> Ma del suo corso momentaneo resti
> Vestigio eterno in dirupati sassi.
>
> (XX, 93)

He brought great but brief aid to the weary and fearful Saracens. You would say that a great but brief bolt of lightning suddenly rushed over and passed, but there remains of its momentary passage, an eternal vestige in broken stones.

The poet implies that the word "grande" applies to both Solimano and Argante as it does to elemental forces of nature or magnificent predatory animals. Such analogies shape our sense of their grandeur and qualify our responses to the kinds of heroism they reveal. By constant comparison to beasts of prey or to whirlwinds, storms, lightning, or to the vast terrors of the ocean, Tasso transforms them into figures of a barbaric, primitive, and unredeemed nature. He juxtaposes these patterns of imagery, based as they are on Homeric similes, to equally pervasive classical allusions, to make a language for characters who embody classical values and standards for the heroic life. In so doing, he shapes our response to the classical heroic ideal that this poem evokes as its past. Tasso allows us to admire heroism of the ancient mold, and moves us by the tragedy to which it inevitably leads. But he ultimately finds it wanting as an image of the heroic life. The values to be derived from classical epic literature bring "grande ma breve aita" to the scene of heroic effort. They leave "vestigio eterno in dirupati sassi," but they must be defeated.

In these figures, Tasso as a creator of Christian epic comes to terms with the legacy of values and ideals expressed in the ancient literature to which he is drawn by his own literary and moral allegiance to "disciplina". He deliberately models episodes, language, and characters, on the conventions established in ancient epic tradition, in the effort to achieve a poem that will evoke the responses of epic. The reader's sense of the classical past shadowing these great figures in the poem contributes a great deal to the power of their heroism and tragedy. Yet the moral qualification of their grandeur inheres in its very creation. They are not only aided by demons, but share a classical language with them. Tasso associates them inevitably with the powers of evil. He will not separate the greatness of the ancient past from the most primitive, unredeemed nature.

The pagans fail. Their tragedy is subsumed in the victory of the Christians. Tasso envisions a more complete heroism into which he incorporates a qualified version of the heroic life they represent. For the Christians, the ancient heroism based on an ethic of personal integrity, honor, and dignity above all else becomes more a temptation than an ideal. A wounded dignity of this kind, for instance, leads Rinaldo to leave the Christian camp in Canto V, and therefore ultimately causes the insuperable magic of the enchanted forest. The most essential fact about the "ancient heroes" in the poem is that they are the enemy, the most formidable individuals on the side of wrong. If a viable heroic ideal is to be created (and this is an essential element of epic as Tasso conceives it), it must incorporate the virtues of the ancient models into a heroic life molded by Christian morality and purpose. Nevertheless, Tasso responds to the power and appeal of the ancient ideal in the undeniable grandeur of these figures. The poet's voice, as it speaks in images of natural force and in the language of the ancient heroic, registers "meraviglia" and tragic pity, revealing the extent of his allegiance to the culture in which his poem finds its sources.

"Meraviglia" and tragic pity also intermingle in the poet's response to the classical heroic that he embodies in the great pagan warriors. It is an admired but devalued ethic. The poet who, in his opening invocation, casts himself in the role of both critic and heir of the classical epic tradition fully expresses that ambivalence in this creation of a classical heroic in the poem. Tasso displays a discriminating mastery over the values and models offered by his understanding of ancient literature. He makes use of the authority infused in poetry through adherence to classical aesthetic principles, but his allegiance to a genuine classical ethic or morality is highly critical. In the poem, as in history, the ancient idea of the heroic is superseded.

4

La Gerusalemme liberata:
The Tragedy of Romance

TASSO'S pagans, heirs of the classical heroic tradition, suffer
defeat at the hands of Christian warriors whose literary ancestry can be traced primarily to romance. But he casts a highly
individual light on these chivalric warriors. Both the poem and his
many discussions of it clearly assert that he intends to establish a
new ideal of a heroic character in "il pio Goffredo," the redeemed
re-creation of "pius Aeneas." From the first description of the
great "capitano" Tasso offers him as an unqualified *exemplum* of
the Christian hero. In contrast to the other warriors in the proces-
sion of heroes in Canto I, he uses no critical language about Goffredo, suggests no inner weakness that could mar his dedication to
the cause. The action begins with God's decree that this figure
should be the supreme commander, ending the delays to the
Crusade. The others, once his "compagni" (chivalric comrades),
are now "ministri" (ministers). As the voice of God on earth, Piero
the Hermit, declares, Goffredo is to be "capo" (head) of an army
that is "un corpo sol de' membri amici" (one single body with parts
agreeing, I, 31). The opening of the poem defines Goffredo's mission—to accomplish the Crusade by bringing back to their true
purposes warriors who must be converted from "compagni" to
"ministri."

When Tasso begins to unfold his story, he presents the internal
weaknesses of the Crusaders themselves as the major obstacles in
their path. His language associates those weaknesses with the tradition of chivalric romance. Goffredo's task was: "sotto a i santi/

Segni ridusse i suoi compagni erranti" (he led his wandering comrades back under sacred banners). As the poet repeats this language
in such passages as Piero's exhortation to the army that they end
the ineffective "governo *errante*" (wavering rule, I, 31), we read in
the phrase "compagni erranti" not only chivalric "knights errant,"
but, in that very character, "erring," wandering from the physical
and moral plane where they belong. The gesture of making Goffredo the sole commander becomes a metaphor for the final goal.
The rest of the epic moves toward its realization in the chivalric
warriors' struggle to adhere to the ideal embodied in Goffredo.
For they are "erranti" through the poem. They act as knights of
romance have traditionally acted, and in so doing, wander away
from their own highest purposes.[1]

This enactment of conflict most engages the imagination of the
poet and our responses as readers, not the marble perfection of the
supreme commander. His fulfillment of the collective vow stands
as the end of the drama and as the abstract standard by which to
judge the great Christian warriors. With this clear, static ideal of
the Christian hero as background, the other Christians, whose
prowess and dedication are essential to the Crusade, occupy the
foreground—Tancredi, with his absorption in a solitary dream of
love, Rinaldo, in his role as "avventuriere" and wanderer to a
mythical island of magic and sensuality. Tasso's concentration on
these characters enriches the poem's representation of heroism by
opening it to the intensely attractive romantic literary tradition.
Their "wanderings" bring into the poem the poetry of love, pleasure, lyric contemplation of emotions and the idyllic face of nature. And they account for most of the poet's "wandering" from
the flow of his narrative and from exclusive concentration on the
vicissitudes of the physical battle. Around these figures the poet
also centers his most complex vision of the Crusade as both physical and moral struggle. It becomes a literal battle for power over an
earthly city, a place historically known and visualized, and a
figurative battle for salvation, for the heavenly Jerusalem.

The union of human and supernatural forces both fulfills Tasso's
theoretical expectation of supernatural machinery in epic, and effectively represents this dual character of the struggle. Tasso
mobilizes nonhuman powers to participate literally in the battle
and also to serve as figures for spiritual states. The effect on the
poem as a whole seems clear at first. The subject of the Christian
crusade against the Moslems of Palestine allows for a clear, uncomplicated moral and narrative structure. The cultural context of the

poem immediately defines its right and wrong elements. Right is the essential attribute of the Christian cause, led by the "pio Goffredo," and wrong characterizes "gl'empi pagani" (the impious pagans). The narrative is, in turn, determined by the moral as well as historical demand that the Christian armies triumph in the poem as they did in actuality. Tasso dramatizes this moral definition of the two sides in the battle and suggests the inevitability of the plot's basic outline, by portraying the supernatural forces arrayed for the struggle. The Christian cause is sanctified by God's direct intervention in its aid, while the union of Plutone and his minions with the opposing forces blackens the pagan cause as automatically as the grimaces and deformity of a morality play villain. History and, more significantly, the moral order of the universe ensure the ultimate Christian victory and give overwhelming strength to the Christian forces in the process of attaining that victory.

Nevertheless, the operation of God and the heavenly spirits in favor of the European invaders does not create an effect of crushing, unopposable power for the forces of good. Nor does the inevitability of the poem's outcome mean that the narrative presents a long, uncomplicated sweep toward victory. The mobilization of spiritual aid demonstrates the difficulty, even impossibility, of a victory for the good without constant, active support from outside the human sphere. Again and again in descriptions of skirmishes and pitched battles, Tasso suggests that the Christians could not conquer without specific divine aid, at that particular moment. In the eighteenth canto, for instance, the pagan defenders of Jerusalem have almost succeeded in destroying the great tower built by the Christians, "e, se più tarda/ Il soccorso del Ciel, convien pur ch'arda" (and if Heavenly aid delays longer, it will surely burn, XVIII, 84). At that moment, the wind suddenly shifts and turns Ismeno's fire back onto the city itself. The syntax of these lines implies that "il soccorso del Ciel" is expected and necessary for that particular situation, and must render aid against a specific danger.

Without divine intervention, the Christian conquest in any moment of the ongoing struggle seems extremely dubious. Fortune rules the battle with her impartial, amoral wheel. Despite the assurance of ultimate victory, the harshness of impersonal destruction dominates the conflict, and the enemy exerts unquestioned power. Supernatural forces supporting the pagans render the forces of evil as universal and many-leveled as the divinely favored good. The human and supernatural forces are constantly balanced.

The poem's structure asserts in effect that good can triumph over evil only after arduous and often dubious battle.

The conditions of battle, revealing human deficiencies in physical and moral power, demonstrate repeatedly that good in the human sphere can be victorious only with constant, particular attention from heaven. Neither the individual heroes nor the whole virtuous army of this epic can summon enough power to achieve their own highest goals alone. God must continually reinforce and redirect them, often in answer to their prayers, and just as frequently without their formal turning to heaven. In a schematic view, the poem's structure dramatizes the Christian idea of grace. It represents in action that infusion of divine power which supplies human weakness with the force to achieve salvation, in whatever form. And in calling on the Virgin as his Muse, Tasso suggests that the poem itself represents an infusion of grace. As a maker of epic, the poet needs power for a poetic conquest parallel to the military and moral victories of its characters.

The possibility of divine grace governs the outcome of the action in the *Gerusalemme liberata*, allowing a victory impossible for man in his fallen state. Within this narrative structure, however, Tasso devotes his greatest attention to that fallen condition itself. The holy warriors need heavenly aid because, to Tasso, the state of being "fallen" essentially means the inability to crush evil. He uses the clash of large armies and the hazards of war, seen en masse, as the literal, physical battle against a visible, external evil. In this outward struggle, he demonstrates by constant, specific interventions from heaven, the weakness of the virtuous side to conquer opposing armies, infernally inspired incantations, magical inventions, or the sheer difficulty of impersonal nature (the Middle Eastern "khamseen" described in Canto XIII). Left alone, human beings are "i miseri mortali" (miserable mortals, XIII, 64). They face a hostile world in which all endeavors, even those against evil, are ruled by the capricious turns of Fortune, and the natural world itself can become an enemy.

But Tasso also conceives of the Crusade as an internal battle. From this point of view, Christian failure to conquer immediately and overwhelmingly results from the presence of affinities to evil within the great warriors, whose complete dedication is necessary for victory. This representation of fallen man depends on a complex sense of the inherent ambiguity in human nature. Tasso projects that sense through the warriors' responses of desire or fear to various manifestations of that evil which they have vowed to destroy, and toward which they should maintain an impenetrable solidity.

In focusing on the psychology of individual characters, Tasso also transforms and deepens the significance of the battle itself. The evil which the Christians have come to conquer is no longer something foreign and external, whose power depends only on the forces it possesses. It becomes instead an essential and constant attribute of individual nature, a part of the divided human psyche. Various elements of the pagan side arouse overwhelming responses in the warriors, responses which vitiate the necessary dedication to their cause. As this cause is identified with their own salvation, the entire plot becomes a representation of the internal crisis of the religious man. The external battle is the catalyst, the scene, the overriding symbol of a psychological conflict with paganism, complicated by the individual's partial allegiance to the forces which he simply rejects on the level of the literal contest.

Through this complexity the epic also becomes the scene of tragedy. A tragic vision of human nature and of human destiny in great endeavors emerges from exploration of individuals dedicated to battle. Yet the main sweep of the narrative, far from marching ineluctably toward tragedy and ruin, moves toward climactic victory. It is meant, like Dante's *Commedia,* to subsume suffering and death in the the transcendent vision of achieved salvation. But when Tasso carries the battle onto the subjective level of individuals dealing with temptations that arouse the most powerful of human emotions, his sensibility dwells on the resulting pain of loss. The internal struggle opens up a profoundly ambivalent vision of human nature making tragedy unavoidable. That vision emerges most completely from the tragedy of Tancredi.

Tancredi is a great warrior, capable of stalemating and eventually killing the formidable Argante. If only as the slayer of two of the three most powerful pagan warriors, he is undoubtedly essential to the success of the Christian cause in a war decided by individual heroism. But from the first we see him troubled and solitary, tortured by an undeclared love for the pagan Clorinda. The poet makes that love an essential part of Tancredi's nature from the first description of him in Canto I:

> . . . e non è alcun fra tanti
> (Tranne Rinaldo) o feritor maggiore,
> O più bel di maniere e di sembianti,
> O più eccelso ed intrepido di core.

S'alcun'ombra di colpa i suoi gran vanti
Rende men chiari, è sol follia d'amore:
Nato fra l'arme, amor di breve vista,
Che si nutre d'affanni, e forza acquista.

(I, 45)

Among so many there is no greater fighter (except Rinaldo) nor one
more beautiful in manner or appearance, nor one more excellent and
high-hearted. If any shadow of guilt makes his great qualities less clear,
it is only the folly of love, a love at first sight, born among arms,
nourished and given power by sighs.

Though more Petrarchan and idealizing than any other in the
poem, this love leads Tancredi away from his "true path" again and
again. He is not "himself"; after Clorinda's death, Piero the Hermit tells him that he has been "da te stesso/ Troppo diverso e da i
principii tuoi" (too far away from yourself and your principles,
XII, 86). Or rather his "self" has become an impossibly ambivalent
entity, torn between the solitary dream of his love and the demands of the communal cause.

The love itself manifests the inclinations of his own nature, for
its object has nothing of the seductive Armida in her. She is "la
donna altera" (the haughty lady, I, 48) who "Armò di'orgoglio il
vólto, e si compiacque/ Rigido farlo" (armed her face with pride
and liked to hold it rigid, II, 39). Only her "onestate," reserve
from men, identifies her with conventional feminine qualities.
Tancredi's burning love arises totally from his own nature's capacity to respond passionately to beauty: "Egli mirolla, ed ammirrò la
bella/ Sembianza, e d'essa si compiacque, e n'arse" (He saw her
and admired her beautiful appearance, was charmed by her and
burned, I, 47).

The view of Tancredi as "da te stesso diverso" also dramatizes
the profound ambivalence of his most ardent allegiances. He is
both Christian hero and lover in essence. Caught in overwhelming
reaction to the presence of his much-contemplated love, he acts in
a manner wholly inconsistent with his role as hero and Christian.
This state of mind and soul is thoroughly comprehensible from the
literary model of the chivalric or Petrarchan lover. But Tasso indicates from the beginning a moral judgment, necessitating some
fatal confrontation between the two forces of the warrior's nature.
Despite his intense absorption in the phenomena of love, the poet
still characterizes this passion as "*follia* d'amore." It moves Tancredi away from his true (morally higher) self. Tasso repeats at

crucial moments of both dramatic representation (Tancredi's declaration of love in III) and discursive judgment (Piero's exhortation
to him in XII), the adjective *smarrito* (lost). He mobilizes all its
Dantesque associations of moral peril and obscurity, by juxtapos-
ing it with images or statements of Tancredi's departure from "la
diritta via" (the right road).

Tasso exploits all the poetic means available to describe and
judge simultaneously this character's course of life. Lyric contemplation, suspended out of time (as in Canto I), reveals him as a
lover of tender reserve with subtle affinities to Erminia. "Così vien
sospiroso, e così porta / Basse le ciglia e di mestizia piene" (So he
comes sighing, with eyelids lowered, full of sadness, I, 49). Within
the narrative context, the poet dramatizes this strange passivity of
what should be an aggressive, heroic nature in the series of encounters with Clorinda. When she attacks him in Canto III, "percosso,
il cavalier non ripercote" (struck, the knight does not strike back).
He loses his nature of "cavaliere" in the emotions of the lover.
Later, he literally deserts his own army to follow an enemy of his
beloved. Even more dramatically, Tancredi is paralyzed by the
sight of Clorinda as he prepares to respond to Argante's challenge
in Canto VI. In the earlier encounter, a momentary image of immobility suggests Tancredi's initial response, "lei veggendo,
impètra" (seeing her, he becomes like stone, III, 23), a graphic
contrast to his behavior as a committed warrior within the Christian army: "Allor, sì come turbine si scioglie, / E cade da le nubi
aereo fuoco, / Il buon Tancredi . . . / Sua squadra mosse . . ."
(Then, like lightning loosed and airy fire fallen from the clouds,
good Tancredi moved his squadron, III, 16). In Canto VI Tasso
expands the image of paralysis to the complete overthrow of all
ordinary expectations about the hero's answer to a chivalric challenge: "Poscia immobil si ferma, e pare un sasso; / Gelido tutto
fuor, ma dentro bolle: / Sol di mirar s'appaga, e di battaglia / Sembiante fa che poco or più gli caglia" (Then he stands immobile and
looks like a stone, completely icy outside but boiling within. He
longs only to look and seems to care little or nothing for battle, VI,
27). Argante's taunts fall with no effect. Tancredi is "attonito quasi
e stupefatto" (as though amazed and stupefied, VI, 28). When he
finally does give battle to Argante, he acts like a man suddenly
awakened from a deep sleep: "Si scote allor Tancredi, e dal suo
tardo / Pensier, quasi da un sonno, al fin si desta" (Tancredi rouses
himself then and finally awakes from his slow thought, as though
from sleep, VI, 30). Tasso offers these images of immobility to

manifest physically a total loss of external consciousness. Tancredi
presents the aspect of a sleeping man, whose whole life is concentrated on the inner vision of a dream, "ma dentro bolle."

The familiar antithesis of Petrarchan images, "Gelido tutto fuor,
ma dentro bolle," takes on very special significances from the context of sleep and dream imagery surrounding Tancredi's love.
Throughout the intermittent narrative of their encounters, there
constantly recurs a language suggestive of dreams and the suspension of ordinary reality that accompanies them. Tancredi first sees
Clorinda when he is "stanco" (weary) and "Cercò di refrigerio e di
riposo" (sought refuge and rest, I, 46). She breaks into his circle of
calm repose, inexplicably abrupt as an apparition. "Quivi a lui
d'improvviso una donzella/ Tutta, fuor che la fronte, armata apparse" (Here suddenly a maiden, totally armed except for her face,
appeared, I, 47). The suspension of the verb (apparse) until the end
of the second line makes it the climax of the sentence. The repetition of this language of magical appearance, juxtaposed to images
of Tancredi's paralysis in a sleeplike trance, reinforces the atmosphere of the extraordinary. The poet's expressions of wonder
break out in close connection with such phrases as "Ecco d'improvviso" (Behold suddenly) and "apparse" (appeared). In III, 21,
for instance, the blow which knocked off Clorinda's helmet is
"Mirabil colpo" (marvelous blow), because "Giovane donna in
mezzo'l campo apparse" (a young woman in the midst of the
battlefield appeared). Two stanzas later, Tancredi has recognized
her, and is immobilized in looking at her. The almost total silence
that reigns throughout their relationship contributes to the dreamlike quality. Despite the few words they speak when Tancredi
begins to declare his love, the image of their meetings in a reader's
mind always includes the silence and distance of intangible beings,
broken only in the death struggle. Tasso represents the idea that
Tancredi's love removes him from his ordinary, real self and from
the path to which he should be dedicated, in language associated
with visually and psychologically extraordinary states, states in
which one is apart from conscious reality.

In the context of this poem, however, such language of extraordinary visions, resembling the dreams of a deep, intense sleep, is
also associated with an ever-present world of magic. The characteristic quality of "apparition" in Clorinda creates subtle rever-
berations from the atmosphere surrounding the seductive
sorceress, Armida. The chaste and distant Clorinda, with her concentration on military valor, seems to dwell worlds apart from the

magical machinations of Armida. But Tasso surrounds the warrior maiden with images that find their referents in the deceptive world of phantasms as much as in the comparatively tangible, familiar experience of sleep and dreams.

These two currents of language actually merge in the description of Rinaldo's temptation. The narrator prefaces his removal to a sensual paradise by descent into a magically invoked and extraordinarily profound sleep, an "image of death" (XIV, 65). Later, when Rinaldo looks at his effeminately adorned image in the bright shield held up by Ubaldo and Carlo, he is "Qual uom, da cupo e grave sonno oppresso, / Dopo vaneggiar lungo in sé riviene" (like a man, weighed down by dark and heavy sleep, who comes back to himself after long wandering, XVI, 31). His sojourn with Armida becomes a long dream.

The echoes created by similar currents of imagery surrounding Tancredi and Clorinda would further render moral judgment on Tancredi's rapt state of love and wonder at the apparition of his image of beauty. But Tasso creates a somewhat different character for Tancredi's love. In Rinaldo, succumbing to love represents a transient forgetting of the warrior's true nature, symbolized in the condition of sleep. Once awakened, he no longer responds to dreams. This allows him to conquer not only this specific temptation, but all other magic and evil opposing the victory of Christianity and his own salvation. He can cast off the dream, and, in this poem, that means freeing himself from the temptation of evil. This is the basis for the creation of an ideal, and leaves no room for tragedy.

But in Tancredi we must understand the response to dream, the sleeplike trance in which he concentrates only on the vision of beauty, as an essential element of his nature, not a mere forgetting of himself. For this character the temptation to eccentric directions corresponds to an internal condition of his being. As I have noted, his love for Clorinda resembles the Petrarchan poet's adoration of a much contemplated and idealized image more closely than any other in the epic. Tasso's insistence on her "altezza," her reserve and distance, only removes Tancredi's love further from such a simple definition as that of a sensual man conquered by the seductive temptress. She does nothing to fan the flames of his passion. The intensity of that passion results from his own nature's capacity to respond to a vision of beauty.

Tasso lays the foundation for a tragedy generated by the essential ambivalences of human nature. But by associating Tancredi's

passionate love for the greatest beauty he can see with a language of
magical apparitions and dreamlike trances of the hero's consciousness, Tasso redefines the nature of the conflict. Love as the content
of dream, as much as sensual temptation, leads the poet to consider
it divergence from the path to salvation. This is particularly true
for the presentation of Tancredi. Rinaldo's dream is "cupo e
grave," so heavily sensual that he can reject it almost automatically
once he becomes aware. In Tancredi, however, the conflict does
not lie between the active path of duty and an obviously undesir-
able satiation of the senses. He is torn instead between his warrior's need for action in the great communal cause and the solitary
reverie of his imagination. By surrounding this contemplative passivity of Tancredi's with a language of sleep and dream, magic and
fantasy, Tasso defines the dream itself as temptation. In his most
intensely delineated conflict, he points the struggle against man as
he dreams, as he imagines overwhelming beauty and loves that
image to the exclusion of all else.

The impossibly ambivalent character of Tancredi's internal battle determines the final culmination of this love in Canto XII.
Clorinda's fatal hour comes in a nightmare of total darkness, in
which each literally fights to the death with nothing of chivalric
dignity or rational skill. In abandoning oneself to pleasurable
dreams, one no longer, as the sage hermit reminds Rinaldo in
Canto XVII, gives reason "il governo" (rule). Instead, one allows
the passional self a freedom to overwhelm the entire spirit. Tancredi's obsession with Clorinda creates a dream world around him,
in which reason, the supreme "capitano" of the heroic life, is swept
away by the demands for satisfaction rising from his impassioned
imagination. Consequently, the darkness, the surrounding silence,
the ironic meeting of the two, drawn into battle by the blind
chance that Clorinda disguised herself—all seem completely appropriate to the moral confusion in which Tancredi's love throws
him. Yet all this further reinforces the identification of that confusion with the dreamlike state, in which passions are undisciplined
and free.

Tasso does not, however, indicate that this battle represents a
conquest of reason over passion, like Rinaldo's. Tancredi's struggle occurs in much vaguer regions of almost unconscious instinct,
proceeding with a primeval violence and blind hate: "Toglie
l'ombra e'l furor l'uso de l'arte. . . . Dansi co' pomi, e infelloniti e
crudi,/ Cozzan con gli elmi insieme e con gli scudi . . ." (Darkness
and fury remove their habitual skill. . . . They hit each other with

crude, vicious blows of their fists, crash their helmets and shields together, XII, 55, 56). In the darkness of the night and their fury, the inevitable tragic outcome of Tancredi's divided nature is both figured and facilitated. If the hero is to operate as a Christian warrior, the spell of contemplated beauty must be broken. The distraction of love and its trance of inward concentration, isolating the spirit from the outside world, cannot exist for Tasso in the same nature that accomplishes great deeds and achieves its salvation. But in the light of day Tancredi could not even touch his love, let alone kill her. Tasso's inexorable demand that the warrior's dream be sacrificed to the restoration of virtuous integrity is, and can only be, expressed in a blind, fate-driven, savage scene of destruction, in which none of the lover's consciousness can possibly participate. For this love has been, from the first, essential to the characterization of Tancredi. Its destruction means the murder of part of himself. Tragedy results inevitably from the perception of conflict within the individual, paralleling the epic confrontation of large historical forces.

The importance of this tragedy to the poetic experience in *La Gerusalemme liberata* emerges most clearly in the portrayal of Tancredi's reaction to his own act of destruction. The poet involves us most intensely in the pain of loss, the pitiful and awful spectacle of one who has been led by a dark fate to kill what he loved best. Tasso focuses his most powerful poetry on Tancredi's lament and self-destructive frenzy. In contrast, the moralizing of Piero the Hermit falls weakly. Nevertheless, Tasso must and does assent to the moral judgment on Tancredi's love and the grief it now inspires. It is right that "A gli atti del primiero ufficio degno/ Di cavalier di Cristo ei ti rappella" (this [loss] recalls you to deeds worthy of the first duty of a warrior of Christ, XII, 87). But in his subsequent portrayal of Tancredi's spirit the poet continues to dwell on pain, not on the Hermit's view of it as "seconda avversità" (favorable adversity). He can only imagine Tancredi obeying the Hermit's exhortation through the fear of damnation: "e in colui de l'un morir la téma/ Poté de l'altro intepidir la voglia" (in him fear of one death [of the soul] could weaken his desire for the other [suicide], XII, 89). The acuteness of emotion is not eliminated, but transformed into dream. In death as in life, Clorinda appears to him as a vividly contemplated, distant vision on which he concentrates in a senseless trance. Yet now her appearance depends totally on his own nature's capacity to dream, to imagine, for she is, in actuality, a dream. "Ed ecco, in sogno, di stellata veste/ Cinta gli appar la sospirata amica" (Behold, in a dream, his longed-for beloved appears clothed in a starry robe, XII, 91).

Though Tasso uses dreams as instruments of revelation to his wholly virtuous characters, Tancredi's dream of Clorinda and the comfort he derives from it are fraught with ambivalence. Despite Tasso's search for a purification of the love image in the baptism of Clorinda at her death, and in Tancredi's dream of her virtuous counsel to him, he cannot really reconcile this dream of love with the role of Christian warrior. He associates that Petrarchan longing for a union in imagination and death too closely with Tancredi's failure in the face of the false illusions of the enchanted forest: "Ma lui, che solo è fievole in amore, / Falsa imago deluse e van lamento" (But he, who is weak only in love, was deluded by a false image and a worthless lament, XIII, 46). The imagination, free from the discipline of reason and the demands of actuality, is always a temptation, a path away from salvation. But the poet's intense participation in the pain of loss, his lingering over Tancredi's imaginings and "sospiri," reveal his own profound attraction to that which he feels must be destroyed. Tragic emotion arises not only from the abstract contemplation of a man killing what he loves, but also from its necessity, from the awful fact that salvation, for Tasso, demands a completely austere, narrow direction of the mind.

> Signor, non sotto l'ombra in piaggia molle
> Tra fonti e fior, tra Ninfe e tra Sirene,
> Ma in cima a l'erto e faticoso colle
> De la virtù riposto è il nostro bene.
> Chi non gela, e non suda, e non s'estolle
> Da le vie del piacer, là non perviene.
>
> (XVII, 61)

Lord, not in the shade on lovely shores among fountains and flowers, Nymphs and Sirens, but at the summit of the steep, wearying mountain of virtue is our good to be found. Whoever neither freezes, nor sweats, nor avoids the paths of pleasure, will not arrive there.

Yet the narrative, rather than establishing moral distance from Tancredi's struggle, suggests an intimate connection between his loss and the very process of creation. Here the theme of dream and free imagination involved in Tancredi's tragedy becomes essential. Tasso almost compulsively associates the language of dream and magic, of imagination and poetry, with love, beauty, sensual temptation. And these throw the most difficult obstacles in the austere path up "l'erto e faticoso colle de la virtù." But what Tasso's morality here condemns also powerfully attracts him as a creator of poetry. In his experience, the poetic imagination, left free to respond to the demands of the passions, inevitably constructs dreams of women, of love and beauty, of impossible yet ardently desired sensual fulfillment. In the language around Tancredi, he identifies love with dream and with the power of the undisciplined imagination.

What this means to him as a poet we can see in the episode of Rinaldo's temptation. There his characterization of a hero who can completely resist evil when the time comes, seems to leave him free to express his ambivalent imaginative inclinations as fully as possible. The sheer quantity of luxuriant, overwhelmingly sensual invention, the lingering over every variation on the theme of eternal spring, and the reprise of the same kind of poetry in the enchanted forest, reveal the poet's intense affinity for this kind of creative act. It is impossible not to feel a power and beauty of poetic capacity, equaled only in the tragic culmination of Tancredi's love. Yet this poetry, so close to his own earlier work, is the dream of a "cupo e grave sonno," through which virtue must walk "rigida e costante" (rigid and constant, XVI, 17). For man as a dreamer, Tancredi in his trance of inward reverie, opens himself to the ungoverned rule of passion, passion which is acceptable only as the disciplined energy of a pure warrior of Christ.

Tasso insists that the wide-ranging emotions of free invention, of ungoverned fantasy, must be subjected to the demands of actuality. Poetry must discipline itself into an effective representation of a reality determined by history and religion. He allows the romantic poetry of chivalric love to live in his poem, but as part of a tragic design in which the character destroys it. He connects the inevitable and necessary tragedy of Tancredi's loss to the poet's sacrifice through the language of dream and imagination. His representation of the hero's pain at having destroyed what he loves best provides some measure of the price the poet pays for the disciplining of his imaginative capacity. Through this sympathetic character, Tasso finds a mode of expression for a poetic tragedy of internal conflict, conflict which he can resolve only by suppressing one side of the ambivalence. The sense of man's fallen state, necessitating an infusion of divine grace to achieve salvation, becomes a condition of poetic as well as historical achievement. The poem itself presents a vision of inevitable ambivalence in human endeavor, analogous to the destinies of the main characters. And in Tancredi, Tasso reveals the tragedy suffered by such a divided nature, even on the way to victory.

5

La Gerusalemme liberata:
The Redemption of Romance

TASSO answers the challenge of romance primarily through the characters of Tancredi and Rinaldo. But he does not merely combine two traditions, aligning them without any thematic or stylistic effect on one another. His effort to make an integrated structure out of epic and romance, in accordance with his theory, results in his self-discipline as a poet of romance, while representing the conversion of romantic characters. More generally, his vision of his poetic goal in the famous "unity in variety" passage of the *Discorsi* flowers in the *Gerusalemme liberata* as an attempt to create a redeemed heroic. The values of both ancient epic and chivalric romance work against each other and against the Christian ideal introduced through the supernatural and historical dimensions of the poem. Both Tasso's individual sensibility and his intellectual allegiance to the demands of his culture bind him to include all these strands of tradition. He also struggles for coherence, for the unity in which every element is linked to every other element by necessity or verisimilitude. Therefore, the romance tradition embodied in the episodes is constantly judged against the literary values of the main plot. The poet weighs the conventional adventures and loves of knights-errant against the austerity of Goffredo and the necessities of the communal cause. Moreover, this is not just any battle for power and glory, but a Crusade for Jerusalem, with all the metaphorical weight those two ideas have acquired through centuries of Christian literature. Wanderings away from this battle in the pursuit of gratification of the passions transform the nature of the battle itself. It becomes both literal and metaphorical. Tasso's heroic poetry takes on an interior emphasis, a psychological thrust that gives his poem a highly original position in the heroic tradition.

Tasso creates a vision of heroic action arising from transcendence of the moral conflicts in which his great Christian warriors struggle for the major part of the poem. Those heroes of romance, Tancredi and Rinaldo, whose dramatic development contrasts with the static perfection of the Christian hero, Goffredo, also come to embody a Christian ideal. Tancredi emerges from tragedy and the moral paralysis of the enchanted wood. He suffers defeat by a false image of a wounded Clorinda and the deceptive sound of her voice in lament, forcibly confessing to Goffredo, "vinto mi chiamo" (I call myself conquered, XIII, 49). But he achieves a salvation in heroic action when he defeats Argante, one of the most formidable forces on the pagan side.

In their final duel, Tancredi confronts an Argante still characterized as the ancient hero: "Più che morir temendo esser respinto;/ E vuol, morendo, anco parer non vinto" (Fearing defeat more than death, and he wants, while dying, still to appear unconquered, XIX, 1). With his usual ferocity of language, Argante taunts Tancredi for violating their common code of honor. He mocks his Christian opponent with his failure to return to their single combat at the appointed time and with his return in an army, not alone. Most effectively, he goads him with the death of Clorinda; "Ché non potrai da le mie mani, o forte/ De le donne uccisor, fuggir la morte" (You who will not be able to flee death at my hands, O powerful killer of women, XIX 3). Tasso achieves a climax of rhetorical finesse by ending this sarcasm with a couplet whose enjambement on "forte" gives sufficient emphasis to what sounds like a complimentary adjective to make the sarcastic accusation crash even more powerfully against Tancredi's vulnerability. But Tancredi has overcome his *bouleversement* at the mention of Clorinda. Tasso creates for him a rhetoric of fierce audacity equal to Argante's: "Vienne in disparte pur tu ch'omicida/ Sei de' giganti solo e di gli eroi:/ L'uccisor de le femine ti sfida" (Come aside you who are the killer only of giants and heroes. The killer of women challenges you, XIX, 5).

In the duel, the characters of the two warriors converge and intermingle. Tancredi reveals himself as a warrior in the grand style (XIX, 7) and Argante, in his moment of contemplative suspension, takes on some of the lyric solitude of the "poetic" Tancredi (XIX,

10). The Christian confronts the pensive Argante with sarcastic taunts similar to those offered to him by his savage opponent in previous episodes. In this last of the virtuoso duels of the poem, where Tasso is at pains to exploit his knowledge of technique, he presents both warriors as fighters of "arte" (skill), as "schermitori" (fencers). He then reduces them both to the most brutal trial of animal strength by their similarity in skill and endurance (XIX, 19). Tancredi, as victor, demonstrates his ability to triumph in the element of pure physical power and martial prowess—like an ancient hero. At this moment, in fact, Tasso chooses to describe him as Hercules battling "the great giant" (XIX, 17). But he is also, in this duel, a hero of chivalric courtesy:

> Tancredi, che'l vedea co'l braccio essangue
> Girar i colpi ad or ad or più lenti,
> Dal magnanimo cor deposta l'ira,
> Placido gli ragiona, e'l piè ritira:
>
> —Cedimi, uom forte; o riconoscer voglia
> Me per tuo vincitore, o la fortuna:
> Né ricerco da te trionfo o spoglia:
>
> (XIX, 20–21)

Tancredi, who sees him striking blows more and more slowly with his exhausted arm, releases the anger from his noble [*magnanimo*] heart and speaks to him calmly, moving back: Yield to me, strong man, acknowledge me or fortune as your conqueror. I seek neither triumph nor spoils from you.

To this Argante, of course, responds "terribile . . . più che mai soglia" (more terrible than ever) and "Tutte le furie sue desta" (arouses all his fury). Surrender means "viltà" (cowardice). Tancredi must beat him down, until this "uom forte" falls through the force of his own blow:

> Per te cadesti; avventuroso in tanto,
> Ch'altro non ha di tua caduta il vanto.
>
> (XIX, 24)
>
> . . . .
> Moriva Argante, e tal morìa qual visse;
> Minacciava morendo, e non languìa.
> Superbi, formidabili e feroci
> Gli ultimi moti fûr, l'ultime voci.
>
> (XIX, 26)

You fell beaten by yourself; so valorous that no other can boast of your fall.

Argante was dying and he died as he lived. He threatened while dying and did not languish. Proud, formidable, fierce were his last motions, his last words.

This final emphasis on Argante's heroic integrity, made all the more dramatic by the narrator's sudden direct address, creates a coherent image of what Tancredi has defeated, the pagan ethic of personal honor and fidelity to one's code to the death. Tasso incorporates this idea of greatness in his Christian hero by using an identical language of battle for both fighters. But Tancredi also commands the voice of chivalric courtesy, of "pietà." And the narrator immediately directs our attention away from the fact of battle to its purpose: "Ripon Tancredi il ferro; e poi devoto / Ringrazia Dio del trïonfale onore" (Tancredi sheathes his sword and then devoutly thanks God for this triumphant honor, XIX, 27). The close spatial alliance in the poetic line of "il ferro" and "devoto," "Dio" and "onore" imitates the quality of heroic action Tasso would make triumphant in the poem.

Tasso embodies this redirection of traditional military valor and chivalric "gentilesse" more fully in the poetry of Rinaldo. Rinaldo incarnates the spirit of the whole crusading army, the body executing the conceptions formed by the head (a divinely inspired Goffredo).[1] Moreover, he is indispensable to the achievement of the crusade on the literal level. We learn this explicitly in Goffredo's vision in XIV:

Perché, se l'alta Providenza elesse
Te de l'impresa sommo capitano,
Destinò insieme ch'egli esser dovesse
De'tuoi consigli essecutor soprano.
A te le prime parti, a lui concesse
Son le seconde: tu sei capo, ei mano
Di questo campo; e sostener sua vece
Altri non pote, e farlo a te non lece.

A lui sol di troncar non fia disdetto
Il bosco c'ha gli'incanti in sua difesa;
E da lui il campo tuo che, per difetto
Di gente, inabil sembra a tanta impresa,
E par che sia di ritirarsi astretto,
Prenderà maggior forza a nova impresa;

E i rinforzati muri, e d'Orïente
Supererà l'essercito possente.

(XIV, 13–14)

For, if high Providence chose you supreme captain of the enterprise, it also destined him to be chief executor of your plans. To you are given the first offices, to him the second. You are the head, he the hand of this army. No other can take his place and it is not permitted to you to do so.

To him alone it is not forbidden to cut down the wood defended by enchantments. Your army which, for lack of people, seems unable to accomplish the great enterprise, and appears forced to retreat, will take greater force from him for new battle. He will conquer the strong walls and the powerful army of the East.

The indispensability of Rinaldo is essential to the coherence in plot for which Tasso strives. It allows him to achieve "unità" despite all the "varietà" which Rinaldo's "wanderings" from the true path bring into the poem. Several letters to the revisers clarify the degree to which Tasso self-consciously engaged himself with this problem. He cites Homeric precedent, as well as theoretical justification, for the inability of the rest of the army to make significant progress without the aid of the body's right arm. At the same time he maintains the necessity of the other warriors for ultimate victory.[2]

Tasso develops this representative figure into a symbol of the inner conflict that the Crusade comes to signify. He creates in Rinaldo a hero of aspirations and nobility very much in the classical tradition; he is the Achilles of the poem. An extreme sensitivity to personal honor and glory moves him from the outset. He initially departs from the Christian camp in a rage at Gernando's challenge to his honor. At the end of the poem, in the final battle, Tasso appropriates his classical heroic language for Rinaldo, now the untroubled warrior dedicated to battle before all else. With the same imagery of animal ferocity and of the overwhelming force of nature that had characterized Argante and Solimano, he transforms Rinaldo into a monster of death (XX, 54). Now the Christian hero roars through the slaughter like the wind or sea (XX, 58). Like Tancredi, Rinaldo incorporates the military grandeur of the ancient heroic ideal.

In the narrative of this last battle Tasso also constructs narrative events to represent the resolution of the moral battle embodied in Rinaldo. This enables him to achieve a poetic resolution of the conflict between strict dedication to narrative concentrated on the historical theme and indulgence in the more lyric poetry of fantasies of love and pleasure that Rinaldo's "errantry" had allowed him. The lines are drawn before the battle. Goffredo declares that Rinaldo's action on the Christian side is essential to victory: "In te, signor, riposta/ La vittoria e la somma è de le cose" (With you, lord, lies victory and the end of this battle, XX, 11). They are fighting a pagan army with Armida in its midst, a source of discord and disunity for them as she was for the Christians: "E in mezzo è poi de la battaglia Armida" (And in the midst of the battle is Armida, XX, 22). The word order of the line emphasizes her presence "in mezzo," reinforcing our sense that the battle for Rinaldo, and therefore for the Christian army is against the "Armida" of this world. She is at the heart of the enemy, for the most potent obstacle to the Crusade throughout the poem has been the temptation to an indulgence of the self that pushes a man away from austere dedication to the cause, away from action and the community of religion through sensual idyll, individual "poetic" fantasies, or a self-centered code of honor. Rinaldo reveals mastery of himself in his ability not only to act as the unrelenting warrior of supreme skill, but to pass by Armida in the midst of the battle: "E fa sembiante d'uom cui d'altro cale" (And he had the appearance of a man to whom other things matter, XX, 62). When Armida launches an arrow at him[3] his armor is impregnable:

> Duro ben troppo a feminil saetta,
> Che, di pungere in vece, ivi si spunta.
> Egli le volge il fianco; ella, negletta
> Esser credendo, e d'ira arsa e compunta,
> Scocca l'arco più volte, e non fa piaga,
> E mentre ella saetta, amor lei piaga.

(XX, 65)

Much too hard for a woman's arrow, which instead of piercing him, is blunted there. He turns aside from her; she, believing herself despised, burning and anguished with anger, shoots with her bow many times; she does not wound him, but while she shoots, love wounds her.

The poet describes a physical act of war that also reveals a moral state. Rinaldo cannot be touched by Armida's weapons. In using a language conventionally manipulated in love poetry as imagery for states of feeling ("saetta," "piaga," etc.), Tasso has converted the traditional language of love lyrics to the service of narrative. It is as though the language of romance, like Armida herself later in the canto, could be redeemed as an element in heroic narrative, because the heroic has expanded through the confrontation with romance. Because of the incorporation of romance material into the traditional military themes of epic, the battle has become both literal and a metaphor for inner conflict. Tasso achieves this depth primarily through the poetry of Tancredi and Rinaldo.

Rinaldo's adventures resemble most closely the sensual, magical and far-flung escapades of the knights-errant in Ariostan romance. Through Rinaldo's "errantry" from "la diritta via" Tasso creates the kind of poetry that constitutes the greatest temptation to him as a poet.[4] This temptation is related to Tasso's theoretical position on the unity within variety proper to epic.[5] By insisting on the God-poet analogy in the *Discorsi*, Tasso not only opens up his conception of epic to allow full scope for his own inclusive allegiances, but actually offers to himself as poet a variety as vast as the cosmos. The problem becomes one of integration and coherence, which Tasso makes clear in the *Discorsi* and in many letters about specific instances in the poem.[6] Tasso's most eloquently stated theoretical position leads him to envisage "an extreme form of tension between variety and unity,"[7] which comes to full fruition in the poem. He reflects that tension thematically in his representation of the obstacles to fulfillment of the Crusade. His warriors are tempted by diverse, individualistic goals and responses. They are led away from the unity of the communal cause by their own variety of character and by the multiple directions in which they are pulled by inner conflict. And the narrative reveals a parallel theme in its self-reflection on the process of composition itself. Tasso reconciles the conflicting narrative demands of unity and variety by allowing scope, but disciplined scope, to potentially contradictory poetic modes. He labors to shape diverse languages into a fully synthesized whole, avoiding the continual perils of disintegration or narrow exclusion.

Tasso turns for variety to those particular parts of the literary cosmos embodied in classical epic and vernacular romance, led there both by his theoretical argument and by his own sensibilities. The "liberating" of Jerusalem becomes a metaphor for the liberation of the poet through the resolution of tensions generated by the confrontation between epic and romance traditions and the Christian ideal. In the course of the poem, epic—the ordered, rationally justifiable, coherent structure—seems to be identified with the poet's adherence to the basic historical, military theme. But Tasso deepens this historical theme so that it also becomes a moral theme through the confrontation with romance. The incorporation of romance leads to a poetry of love, to scenes literally removed far from the field of battle, inviting a language of hedonistic enjoyment of nature and sensuality. As a result, both the poet's adherence to epic narrative structure and the characters' dedication to the struggle for Jerusalem come to signify allegiance to God and Christian morality. Tasso modifies the very nature of the heroic poem. Heroic action means both a literal, historically known fight—a physical battle for a geographical city—and an inner struggle for mastery over the powerful attraction of the passions and freely roaming individuality.

This dual sense of the heroic emerges from the poem as a whole through the juxtaposition of episodes, conversations, patterns of imagery, narrative description, and comment. But in some parts of the poem Tasso moves toward a language that expresses this dual vision by asking the reader to respond to it as both literal and figurative. We find such a language primarily in the poetry around Rinaldo. The first major episode of this sort is the enchanted forest of Canto XIII. Tasso makes this enchanted forest the main obstacle to the Christian conquest. Without the wood it supplies, the Crusaders cannot construct the siege machinery necessary to take the city. But they are unable to overcome its terrors without Rinaldo, the only Christian capable of defeating this mysterious enemy. As a result, they cannot achieve the goal of the Crusade until Rinaldo is reunited with his comrades.

Tasso creates this forest in great detail, with a language richly evocative of the mystery and terror to which he is characteristically drawn. Before he even describes the fearful magic by which Ismeno enchants the woods, he makes it a place of darkness: "Che rassembra infernal, che gli occhi ingombra / Di cecità, ch'empie di téma il core" (that seems infernal, burdening the eyes with darkness, filling the heart with fear, XIII, 3). No shepherd or herdsman ever enters there, nor "peregrin, se non smarrito" (wayfarer, if not lost, XIII, 3). And with this association to the "selva oscura" in which another "peregrin" found himself "Che la diritta via era smarrita" (Inferno, Canto I), the language of the forest immediately takes on an element not only of subjective reaction, but of moral significance to which narrative description is always pointing. As Tasso describes what happens to the Christians in their attempt to enter the forest, he talks about psychological states. The enchantment works by creating overwhelming re-

sponses of fear within the warriors. The major obstacle to the
conquest of Jerusalem becomes the inability of men to conquer
their own inner being.

The poet insists that the terrors of the forest are a matter of
appearance. The artisans are the first to be quelled.:

> Qual semplice bambin mirar non osa
> Dove insolite larve abbia presenti,
> O come pave ne la notte ombrosa,
> Imaginando pur mostri e portenti;
> Così temean, senza saper qual cosa
> Siasi quella però che gli sgomenti;
> Se non che'l timor forse a i sensi finge
> Maggior prodigi di chimera o sfinge.

> (XIII, 18)

Like a simple child who dares not look where strange ghosts seem to
appear or who is frightened in the gloomy night imagining monsters
and fearsome shapes, so they fear without knowing what it is that
terrifies them. Or perhaps their fear feigns even greater appearances of
chimeras and sphinxes to their senses.

These "larve" leave them "timida e smarrita" (timid and bewildered), unable to carry on the work necessary to achieving the
Crusade. Goffredo's squad of "guerrieri eletti" (chosen warriors,
XIII, 19) are oppressed by "vil timore" (base fears, XIII, 20),
before they even enter the forest. Neither "disciplina" nor "ragion" can defend them against the fear that rises in them when they
merely hear sounds.

The theme of fraudulent appearance is particularly clear when
the poet relates Tancredi's attempt to defeat the enchantment. And
Tancredi's failure reveals most emphatically that the Christians are
being defeated by their own internal weaknesses and affinities to
the temptations offered by evil. The appearance of monsters and
terrifying flames or howling sounds that make the forest like a
"novella Dite" (new Dis) cannot daunt him. But he is overcome by
the sound of Clorinda's voice lamenting and the sight of blood
springing from a tree when he strikes it. The narrator not only
conveys the intensity of Tancredi's internal *bouleversement,* but
responds with him sympathetically ("Pur tragge al fin la spada, e
con gran forza / Percote l'alta pianta. Oh meraviglia! / Manda fuor
sangue la recisa scorza." Finally he draws forth his sword and with
great strength strikes the tall plant. Oh wonder! Blood shoots

forth from the cut bark, XIII, 41). Yet he continues to use a
language that judges critically the hero's inability to overcome this
"falsa imago" (false image). He associates the event with the state
of being "smarrita," mobilizing the moral implications created for
that adjective in the *Commedia*. He evokes even more particular
associations to *Inferno*, by comparing the illusory flaming towers
and battlements to "Dite" (*Inferno* VIII, 68) and confronting Tancredi with a bleeding tree from which a lamenting voice is heard,
like the voice of Pier delle Vigne in *Inferno* XIII. Even more
explicitly, he calls Tancredi "l'infermo" (a sick man) who fears
something "in sogno" (in a dream):

> Se ben sospetta, o in parte anco s'accorge
> Che'l simulacro sia non forma vera,
> Pur desìa di fuggir; tanto gli porge
> Spavento la sembianza orrida e fèra
>
> (XIII, 44)

Even if he suspects or partly realizes that the semblance is not a true
being, still he longs to flee, such fear strikes him from the terrible and
savage apparition.

Tancredi's response transforms him from "intrepido" (undaunted)
to "il timido amante" (the fearful lover) yielding to "falsi inganni"
(false deceits). The poet cements the relation between the hero's
defeat here and his bondage to his own passional nature:

> Così quel contra morte audace core
> Nulla forma turbò d'alto spavento;
> Ma lui, che solo è fievole in amore
> Falsa imago deluse e van lamento.
>
> (XIII, 46)

So this heart, bold even against death, was not perturbed by any fearful
form. But he who is only weak through love was deluded by a false
image and an empty lament.

Tasso defines Rinaldo's enterprise in the enchanted forest as the
conquest of man's divided nature. His use of romance conventions
(an enchanted wood, evil magician) within the epic narrative allows him to express the internal dimension of the conflict. He
accomplishes this with even greater complexity in the longest romantic passage in the poem, the search for Rinaldo. He introduces
the episode with a wholly moral language in its prelude, Gof-

fredo's dream (Canto XIV). Rinaldo must come back from his "errore," to which he was led "per soverchio d'ira" (overweening anger). His return to the camp is synonymous with a rededication to true "onore." Now "il giovene delira, / E vaneggia ne l'ozio e ne l'amore" (the youth raves and wastes himself in indolence and love, XIV, 17). The messengers must "liberarlo" (liberate him), so that he may liberate the entire army. His return will mean that he has learned to control his passions and to act in the discipline of the common cause:

> Torni Rinaldo; e da qui inanzi affrene
> Più moderato l'impeto de l'ire,
> E risponda con l'opre a l'alta spene
> Di lui concetta, ed al comun desire.
>
> (XIV, 26)

Let Rinaldo return and henceforward rein in and moderate the fury of his anger, and let him produce deeds corresponding to the high hope conceived of him and to our common desire.

The narrative has already related this achievement of the ideal moral state in the individual to the common salvation. For God answered Goffredo's prayer (in Canto XIII) directly with a new order of things:

> Or cominci novello ordin di cose,
> E gli si volga prospero e beato.
> Piova: e ritorni il suo guerriero invitto,
> E venga a gloria sua l'oste d'Egitto.
>
> (XIII, 73)

Now let a new order of things begin, and turn prosperous and blessed. Let it rain, and let his unconquered warrior return and the Egyptian host come for his glory.

Rinaldo's return is to be both catalyst and symbol of a "prospero e beato" course for the Christian cause. In suggesting an analogy between Rinaldo's reappearance and a beneficent change in nature, the poet sounds a theme that he develops more fully in the description of his hero's rededication on the Mount of Olives.

The total effect of that scene depends, however, on the complex of themes and the quality of language unfolded in the long journey to Armida's garden. Of all the episodes in the poem, this one is most closely linked to romance tradition. Its conventions—the

guides who provide the travelers with information and magic objects, the journey to a mythical island, the monster guardians, and
the whole scene of idyllic pleasure and beauty—are rooted in that
literary world of fantasy so attractive to Tasso as narrative poet. In
his use of that tradition here he not only deepens his heroic narrative through an internal moral dimension, but also confronts the
resulting tensions for poetry itself, for the idea of art and the
responsibilities of the artist.

The narrative constantly asks the reader to respond to figures
and scenes both on the level of literal, narrative description and on
a level of moral interpretation. For instance, the conventional
figure of the guide, the "Mago Naturale" (Natural Magician) gives
Carlo and Ubaldo information and help for their journey. But he
also functions as a quasi-allegorical figure, whose description and
place in the poem's structure create certain generalized moral
ideas. Tasso designed the whole speech of the "Mago Naturale" to
convey the idea that he represents natural reason: "Nacqui io pagan, ma poi ne le sant'acque/ Rigenerarmi a Dio per grazia pia-
cque" (I was born pagan, but then I was regenerated in the holy
waters by the grace of God, XIV, 41). The reader translates his
statements about what he does into a small, conventional treatise
on the proper place of natural reason in human life. He also provides an explicit contrast to the pagan Ismeno's evil knowledge and
manipulation of nature: "Né in virtù fatte son d'angioli stigi/ L'o-
pere mie meravigliose e conte/ (Tolga Dio ch'usi note o suffumigi/
Per isforzar Cocito e Flegetonte)" (Nor are my marvelous deeds
done by the power of stygian angels. God forbid that I should use
incantations or fumes to force Cocitus and Phlegethon, XIV 42).

Tasso's version of the guide remains a rather cut-and-dried
figure of moral and philosophical significance. This way of handling a romance convention is noteworthy, however, because it
introduces the poetic mode of this whole romantic "divergence" in
the poem. Tasso constructs the traditional episodes to be both
valuable in themselves and the means to moral statements. He
invents a poetry of romance with all his capacity for luxuriance and
intensity, and at the same time turns it into a language of the
internal life.

When Carlo and Ubaldo have conquered the fearful monsters
guarding the mountaintop, they win through to an idyllic scene of
softness, sensual pleasure, and all the traditional accompaniments
of satisfied love. The poet allows his imagination to dwell in this
literary zone, describing every element in full detail. Adjectives,

similes, long comparisons and typical events (the "carpe diem" song) all enrich the theme of love and sensual gratification. But as a constant background to this luxuriantly imagined version of the topos, he sketches the secondary theme of moral judgment. The poet never loses control of the full implications of his imagined world. Despite the success with which he evokes a sensual paradise, he constantly reminds us of the necessary evaluation of these scenes by contrasting this world of indulgence with the moral control represented by the warriors. We can experience the interweaving of these two patterns of language in the characters' response to "il fonte del riso" (the fountain of laughter):

> Ecco il fonte del riso ed ecco il rio
> Che mortali perigli in sé contiene;
> Or qui tener a fren nostro desio,
> Ed esser cauti molto a noi conviene;
> Chiudiam l'orecchie al dolce canto e rio
> Di queste del piacer false Sirene;
>
> (XV, 57)

Behold the fountain of laughter and behold the stream [rio] that holds mortal perils. Here we must rein in our desires and we must be cautious. Let us close our ears to the sweet, evil [rio] song of these false Sirens of pleasure.

The symmetry and the play on words of the first line express the intimate connection between this loveliness and "il rio." The placement of the double entendre at the end of the line, where it is echoed in the similarly close connection of *dolce* and *rio* in the fifth line, qualifies any response of simple delight or longing for these scenes of "donzellette garrule e lascive" (chattering, sensual maidens). In fact they have already been characterized as "false Sirene."

Throughout the episode the poet maintains the tension between the pleasure in imagining this scene and the need for a final repudiation of it. He manifests such strain particularly clearly in the constant variations on the love-war theme. Armida's garden is a deliberate alternative to the Crusade. The tantalizing nymphs of the fountain call the two warriors "fortunati peregrin" (fortunate wayfarers), and welcome them to "quel piacer . . . / Che già sentì ne' secoli de l'oro / L'antica e senza fren libera gente" (that pleasure once experienced in the golden ages by the ancient, lawless free people, XV, 63). In this world so closely linked to the *Aminta*, they urge the warriors to give up all thought of heroic action, of the arms that define their natures as epic characters:

> L'arme, che sin a qui d'uopo vi fôro,
> Potete omai depor securamente,
> E sacrarle in quest'ombra a la quïete:
> Ché guerrier qui solo d'Amor sarete;
> E dolce campo di battaglia il letto
> Fiavi, e l'erbetta morbida de' prati.
>
> (XV, 63–64)

The weapons, which were necessary to you until you came here, you can now safely put down and consecrate to peace in this shady place. Here you will be warriors only of Love, and the sweet battlefield is the bed and the soft grass of the meadows.

The playful tone of this "voce dolce e pia" (sweet, gracious voice) allows us for a moment to respond to this imagery of "guerrier d'Amor" as we would to countless traditional love lyrics. But Tasso uses the conventional language of love poetry here both to reveal the nature of the temptation and to establish a perspective that sees this way of talking, this kind of poetry, as temptation. For the idea of changing from real warriors to "warriors of love" is not only metaphor, but an actual possibility. In the context of the poem and of the moral language that serves as prelude to this episode, such a shift in values represents a reenactment of the Fall, a falling away from the true path to salvation. The warriors' response in the next stanza immediately puts this speech of invitation into that moral perspective. The conventional extravagances of love poetry become "vezzi perfidi e bugiardi" (treacherous, lying charms):

> Ma i cavalieri hanno indurate e sorde
> L'alme a que' vezzi perfidi e bugiardi;
> E'l lusinghiero aspetto e'l parlar dolce
> Di fuor s'aggira, e solo i sensi molce.
>
> (XV, 65)

But the warriors have hardened themselves and made their souls deaf to these treacherous, lying charms. The tempting appearance and sweet talk circles around outside them and touches only the senses.

These warriors, for whom "il parlar dolce" remains "di fuor" provide, by their presence, a complete contrast to Armida's magic circle. She has decorated her palace with scenes from famous classical stories of warriors conquered by love, continuing the Mars and Venus motif sounded before. In further development of the garden's classical ambience, Tasso locates it in "l'isole Felici" (Happy Isles) where the men of "la prisca etate" (the first age) had imagined "gli elisi campi" (the Elysian fields). He also identifies the temptresses as "Sirene," making Armida's garden a fully realized vision of the temptation by pagan values. Carlo and Ubaldo exist in polar opposition to this scene of Venus triumphant. Though Armida "si gloria d'impero" (glories in her reign) and Rinaldo loves his state of "servitù" (servitude, XVI, 21), they are "rigida e costante" (upright and constant) "Fra melodia sì tenera, fra tante / Vaghezze allettatrici e lusinghiere" (among such tender melodies, such tempting, soothing beauties, XVI, 17). They serve as the representatives of that other world whose very presence reveals the idyll as "bugiardo" and "perfido." "Ascosi / Mirano i due guerrier gli atti amorosi" (Hidden, the two warriors watch the amorous play, XVI, 19).

By the introduction of their observant yet detached point of view in the great love scene of Rinaldo and Armida, Tasso maintains the contrasting perspective of the warrior's duties, even while the narrative dwells on the intense pleasure of the scene. "Guerrier" is constantly set against "atti amorosi." An aside by the narrator calls the mirror that hangs at Rinaldo's side "estranio arnese" (strange weapon). This "estranio arnese," the pretext for a courtly love-game and an intricate Petrarchan love poetry, opposes the shield-mirror—a real weapon—held up to Rinaldo by those two "rigid and constant" warriors. Reflected in that mirror, Rinaldo as lover, as Mars reclining at the feet of Venus, appears: "Qual feroce destrier ch'al faticoso / Onor de l'arme vincitor sia tolto, / E lascivo marito in vil riposo / Fra gli armenti e ne' paschi erri disciolto" (like a fierce war-horse taken away from the laborious honor of victorious arms, who wanders loose among flocks and herds, a lascivious stallion in base repose, XVI, 28). And in the character of "lascivo marito" the narrator immediately calls him "ebro e sopito" (drunken and stupefied) among soft pleasures.

When Rinaldo looks in that "lucido scudo" (clear shield) he sees himself "con delicato culto adorno" (adorned with exquisite refinement), a phrase that perfectly summarizes the cultivated, refined, artful quality of Armida's garden. The intricate architecture, the entrance through elaborately decorated doors, the landscape so perfect in its pleasures that its total artfulness even includes the pleasure of looking as though there were no art (XVI, 9, 10, 12)—all invite us to understand Armida's garden as a supreme expression of art. The emphasis on art that looks like nature and nature looking like art significantly pervades Tasso's description, though it conventionally characterizes Renaissance descriptions of idyllic or pastoral scenes. Most easily, Tasso's evocation of this motif reinforces our understanding of Armida's garden as a re-creation of the pagan ideal, and of that aspect of the high Renaissance ideal involved with a vision of the golden age.[8]

But the emphasis on the garden's artfulness connects most significantly to the theme of poetry and the artist's responsibilities in the *Gerusalemme* as a whole. For Armida, in the artifice of this idyllic retreat, is identified with the artist, the poet himself. Her magic, like the poet's imagination: "Dié corpo a chi non l'ebbe (gave a body to what had none, XVI, 24). The prominence of this motif in Tasso's garden of sensual pleasure relates the temptations for the hero to the temptations for the poet. This kind of poetry— the language of love and sensuality, of lyric contemplation of beauty and passive introspection ("ozio")[9]—potentially distracts the poet from his higher duty to imagine the way to the achievement of the crusade. When Rinaldo looks in the shield, he sees that even his sword in that atmosphere of "delicato culto" looks "effeminato" (effeminate) from "troppo lusso" (too much luxury). It is so adorned that it seems "inutile ornamento" (useless ornament) rather than "militar fèro instrumento" (powerful weapon of war). While the narrative reveals the hero's new awareness of a dual perspective on himself, it also suggests a confrontation of analogous alternatives for poetry. Tasso had associated the lyric themes of love and repose with the "ornamental" style ("fiorita vaghezza"). From the perspective of this epic they make poetry a frivolous ornament rather than a strong instrument of moral education depicting the truths of human life and the way to redemption.

Through his evocation of the romance world, however, Tasso achieves a redemption of poetic language analogous to the redemption of the hero most essential to the whole army's salvation. His expansion of the perspectives by which these scenes are viewed and evaluated allows the moral dimension to remain constant, despite the attractions of an evocative language. Rinaldo's final awakening arrives as the long-prepared culmination of a pervasive undercurrent of judgment. He returns to the conscious, rational self, after a "vaneggiar" in the world of dreams. Rinaldo has sojourned "fuora/ Del mondo, in ozio" (outside the world in idle repose), with his "virtù" "sopita" (drowsy). The theme of love and war comes to a resounding finale in Ubaldo's speech in which a whole stanza is pointed toward the final phrase of condemnation: "egregio campion d'una fanciulla" (distinguished champion of a girl, XVI, 32). In contrast to the world of "ozio," Ubaldo holds up all of Asia and Europe at war. He reminds Rinaldo of his place in it as "fatal guerriero" (destiny's warrior), whose sword must be "inevitabile," not "inutile ornamento." The constant juxtaposition of the two sets of values throughout the episode prepares and justifies Rinaldo's response to the view of himself in the mirror of the warriors' world. Like a man startled out of "cupo e grave sonno" (dark and heavy sleep), he returns to "himself," to "ragion."

Yet Tasso continues to demonstrate the intense attraction of Armida's world for the poetic imagination in his lengthy treatment of this scene. He reveals his own affinity for a poetry of feeling, of emotional analysis and expression, in the long consideration of Armida's despair and her efforts to restrain the departing hero. He models the scene on sympathetic treatments of abandoned women in heroic literature (Dido and Aeneas, Theseus and Ariadne), finding appropriate representation for the artist's ambivalent response to his hero's departure. It remains, however, a controlled ambivalence. Armida's lament is answered by a Rinaldo who "resiste e vince" (resists and conquers) like Carlo and Ubaldo at the fountain of laughter, because "ragion congelò, la fiamma antica" (reason froze the old flame, XVI, 52).[10] But Rinaldo does not find it necessary to construct defenses against his own attraction by a cold rigidity. Instead of love, "V'entra pietade . . . / Pur compagna d'Amor, benché pudica" (pity enters, the chaste companion of love, XVI, 52). Tasso creates an image of the chivalric hero who responds to the appeal of the emotions, but remains clear about the proper hierarchy of duties: "Sarò tuo cavalier, *quanto concede*/ La guerra d'Asia e con l'onor la fede" (I will be your knight, *inasmuch as* the Asian war and faith with honor will allow me, XVI, 54). The traditional motives for chivalric action, "onor," "cortesia," "pietà" are valued only as they can be incorporated into a wider duty: "Cortesia lo ritien, pietà l'affrena/ *Dura necessità* seco ne'l porta" (Courtesy holds him back, pity restrains him, *harsh necessity* forces him away, XVI, 62; my italics).

The poet redeems romance subject matter and its language by his creation of a moral and psychological dimension within the narrative. Tasso gives new weight to the expression of feelings, the

obstacles resulting from human weakness, which have always
played a part in heroic narrative. By the effort to incorporate
romance into epic in a wholly coherent structure, he opens up the
potentiality for moral or psychological action within the heroic
tradition. The narrative means used to effect Rinaldo's reunion are
particularly significant in this respect. The literal journey itself
occupies very little of the poet's attention. What he exploits most is
the moral perspective operative throughout the episode of Armida's garden.

In the relation of Rinaldo's return, the reader responds constantly to moral implications of events, or the events themselves
exist wholly on a spiritual plane. In the same canto (XVII) in
which the poet presents Rinaldo, in the classical manner, as the
heroic ancestor of a line of illustrious progeny,[11] he redirects our
understanding of such greatness to moral and spiritual ideas. He
accomplishes this through the "Mago Naturale," the representative
of a Stoic wisdom based in the classical past, speaking in a version
of a saying of Simonides.[12] His imagery also refers, however, to
the romance world from which we have just emerged:

> Signor, non sotto l'ombra in piaggia molle
> Tra fonti e fior, tra Ninfe e tra Sirene,
> Ma in cima a l'erto e faticoso colle
> De la virtù riposto è il nostro bene.
>
> (XVII, 61)

Lord, not in the shade on lovely shores among fountains and flowers,
Nymphs and Sirens, but at the summit of the steep, wearying mountain of virtue is our good to be found.

Tasso's poetry has created a literal reality for the "fonti e fior,"
"Ninfe e Sirene." But here we also respond to them as metaphors
for the psychological state of "ozio" or "sogno." Tasso incorporates associations with both the classical heroic tradition and romance into an essentially moral idea of the heroic.

The traditional idea of heroic action also becomes both literal
and metaphorical in the language given to the Mago Naturale.
Rinaldo's heroic qualities are his "spirti generosi, ed alti" (gener-
ous, noble spirits) and his "ire veloci e pronte" (swift, ready ferocity, XVII, 62). They remain heroic as long as they are not
"ministre di desidèri ingordi . . . e da ragion discordi" (ministers of
greedy desires out of harmony with reason), but combat "aversari
esterni" (external adversaries) and "con maggior forza" (with

greater force) "Le cupidigie, empi nemici interni" (the passions, bitter internal enemies, XVII, 63). Rinaldo, he says, must learn to "govern" his passions. The individual must achieve internal control over the army of passions by instituting reason as the sole "duce," just as the external army of the Crusade must acknowledge one captain in authority. From this moralizing voice, we hear explicitly that the battle, for the Christians, is both external and internal. Though such insight remains reductively moralistic when spoken by the *Mago Naturale*, the speech does signal a new stage in the development of the narrative. It reminds us of the opening of the poem, while suggesting the much larger meanings now available for the "errantry" of Goffredo's "compagni" and for the assertion of effective authority over the army.

Piero the Hermit calls Rinaldo "mirabil peregrino" (wondrous wayfarer) who has been "errando" (XVIII, 6); "smarrito agnel" (lost lamb) brought back to God's "gregge" (flock, XVIII, 7). We respond to this language and to everything that happens in the narrative of Rinaldo's return to the army as spiritual events. The language at once literally describes tangible events and creates metaphors for the spiritual transformation of the hero, and through him of the Crusade. In the narrative of Rinaldo's return to the camp at dawn, and his journey to the Mount of Olives, Tasso achieves a language that operates simultaneously in both dimensions. The sense of sublimity and harmony in this episode largely results from a resolution of those artistic tensions that create much of the drama of the poem in a vision of a redeemed life.

The dawn on the Mount of Olives washes the hero clean of "la caligine del mondo / E de la carne" (the soot of the world and the flesh, XVIII, 8), so that he may conquer both "mostri e giganti" (monsters and giants) and all "folle error" (foolish error, XVIII, 10). It exists as a literal event, the ritual form of confession and penance actually accomplished in the flesh. But all the language used to narrate it asks us also to read the event as emblematic of the renewal of faith, the purification of the soul achieved in baptism. The signals for such dual reading begin with the simple recognition that Tasso has chosen the Mount of Olives, with its biblical resonances, as a literal referent for the image of "l'erto e faticoso colle de la virtù." Rinaldo prays that "il mio vecchio Adam purghi e rinovi" (my old Adam be purged and renewed, XVIII, 14). Nature responds with "un rugiadoso nembo" (a dewy cloud) that "l'asperge" (sprinkles him). In answer to his prayer "la rugiada del ciel" (heavenly dew) miraculously purges from his clothes "il pallor" (dullness) and "induce in esse un lucido candore" (creates in them a clear brightness). We are reminded of the "lucido scudo" in which Rinaldo first perceived the nature of his existence.

The description of man and nature here is both literal and symbolic. Reality is transformed by the supernatural in a literal miracle which we also read as spiritual renewal and rebirth. The poet compares that "lucido candore" to the new beauty of "smarrite foglie" (drooping leaves) when "i matutini geli" (morning frosts) touch "arido fiore" (a withered flower). By summoning the adjective "smarrito" to a central position in this simile, Tasso suggests both a concrete reality in nature and simultaneous associations with the constant moral meaning of "smarrito" in this poem and in literary tradition. A further simile links the event to the renewal of the "lieto serpente" (gay serpent) when he adorns himself "di nov'òr" (with new gold, XVIII, 16). The poet conveys in this brief image the fresh energy of this event in nature, traditionally in Christian literature a figure for baptism and the "vita nova" of the "new Adam."

In this vision of reconciliation and forgiveness, Tasso achieves a wholly integrated language of tangible action and spiritual meaning. He turns it to the theme of poetry itself in Rinaldo's contemplation of the nocturnal heaven on his journey to the mountain. The hero still responds to beauty and the poet suspends the movement of the narrative for this moment of contemplation. But the lyric response to beauty and emotion is aroused by "Bellezze incorruttibili e divine" (Beauties that are incorruptible and divine, XVIII, 12). And heroic action here consists in the recognition of the contrast between the "belle luci" (beautiful lights) of the "tempio celeste" (heavenly temple) and the "torbida luce e bruna,/ Ch'un girar d'occhi, un balenar di riso/ Scopre in breve confin di fragil viso" (dark, troubled light, that glancing eyes, a flashing laugh, reveal in the small space of a frail face, XVIII, 13).

These visionary moments establish the context for Rinaldo's conquest of the enchanted forest. The transformed hero confronts a new version of Armida's garden—the "Ninfe e Sirene" (XVIII, 19), the fertile life-giving nature where trees are "feconda" (fertile, XVIII, 26). They give birth to "dee boscareccie" (rustic goddesses) who look like productions of art (XVIII, 27) and perform a pastoral show for him as if part of the *Aminta* were being acted out. To describe these appearances in the forest Tasso again exploits an imagery of "l'antica etade" (the olden times) and moves to its culmination in the "angelica beltade" (angelic beauty) of an image of Armida.

But the poet constantly intersperses his description with the negative judgment conveyed by its "false" quality. It is all "falso aspetto." He makes us see these beauties as potential horrors by transforming the images of Armida and the nymphs into classical monsters. Through all the "vane sembianze" (empty appearances), Rinaldo remains "accorto" (aware, XVIII, 33). His heroism consists in clarity of judgment and the moral strength to ignore what had formerly attracted him. The "cavalier" has developed from a knight-errant to a hero who can be called "venerabile e severo" (venerable and stern), adjectives used characteristically of Piero the Hermit. Tasso associates this heroism with the grandeur of ancient heroes. Rinaldo's statement to Goffredo, "A quel temuto/ Bosco n'andai, come imponesti, e'l vidi:/ Vidi, e vinsi gl'incanti" (I went to that fearsome wood, as you directed me and I saw it; I saw and conquered the enchantments, XVIII, 40), with its classical echoes, connects the moral heroism of his conquest to the greatness of ancient epic characters.

Tasso's heroic ideal depends on his inclusive urge to incorporate the active qualities of both ancient hero and chivalric "cavalier" into a Christian perspective. The embodiment of that ideal in the poetry around Rinaldo results in a new psychological—moral thrust for heroic language.[13] In the poem as a whole this dimension of language, character and structure coexists with the demands of a literal narrative of "high enterprise." The value accorded to the public narrative of actual events cannot be dismissed. The poet recreates an event considered true because it happened in history. In using language that will convey the "meraviglia" of events that happened in a particular time and place, he also expresses the moral and spiritual meaning for all men in all time. Epic has always sought to understand the larger meanings of the conflicts it depicts, constructing ideal visions of the heroic life, dwelling on the greatness of human possibility. Epic poets have always envisioned as heroes men and women who struggle to expand our sense of the human, who push beyond ordinary limits.

But Tasso redirects our understanding of heroic action to the inward and psychological. He raises to a new pitch the potentiality for heroism in inner action, in the mastery over spiritual and moral conflicts. He invents powerful images for such a heroism, analogous in "meraviglia" to the heroism of ancient epic or traditional romance, in episodes like Rinaldo's conquest of his passion for Armida, his achievement of renewed manhood on the Mount of Olives, or the purely psychological heroic action of the enchanted forest. The poem as a whole projects the sense that heroic poetry springs from the moral life as much as, or more than, "great deeds."

Tasso redefines the enterprise itself through his welding of epic and romance. He retains the value of traditional epic events in his poem. They are not a mere pretext. But his poetry thrusts most strongly toward an interior, psychological sense of heroic narrative. The triumph of the Crusaders' achievement becomes also a triumphant resolution of the conflicting artistic and moral demands embodied in their struggle.

Tasso's poem is not, therefore, a mere conglomeration of elements from distinct traditions—classical epic on one side and romance on the other—huddled together like building blocks. We cannot simply separate the various strands of tradition and examine them for their value and effectiveness, though both Renaissance and modern critics have tended to do so. If we take seriously the structural, thematic and linguistic connections Tasso has achieved, we must recognize their effectiveness in binding the poem into a coherent whole. Though he operated extremely self-consciously in choosing elements of tradition, he has not merely added them to each other, each retaining its original identity and asking for disparate responses. On the contrary, the poem's genuine coherence, achieved out of the tensions of literary and moral oppositions, ends by transmuting tradition into something new. Though Tasso reincarnates the classical heroic in the poem, it lives, both admired and devalued, in a context complicated by its juxtaposition with different heroic codes. The poet similarly recreates and reevaluates the actions and motivations of romance. The *Gerusalemme liberata* reveals that a heroic poem can transform the entire heroic tradition into a metaphor for the inner struggles of the religious man and yet infuse in such psychological action the authority, universality, and at the same time, the concrete validity, of epic.

6

Paradise Lost

TO read Tasso's poem as a significant moment in the long Christian transmutation of classical epic offers the possibility of understanding Milton's intense admiration for this Italian predecessor. That admiration strikes us when we find him citing Tasso as the only noteworthy example of contemporary epic poetry in *The Reason of Church Government,* as he mentions his models for the long epic he hopes to write: "Time servs not now, and perhaps I might seem too profuse to give any certain account of what the mind at home in the spacious circuits of her musing hath liberty to propose to her self, though of highest hope, and hardest attempting, whether that Epick form whereof the two poems of Homer, and those other two of Virgil and Tasso are a diffuse, and the book of Job a brief model . . ." (pp. 812–13). Without argument, Milton ranks Tasso with Virgil and Homer, and expects the reader to understand immediately the idea of a literary form exemplified by this group of poems. Tasso, as much as the classical poets, contributes to that cosmopolitan tradition of "the best and sagest things" which Milton would strive to incorporate into his own poetic voice.

Yet modern readers have usually expressed discomfort at this version of the ancestry of *Paradise Lost,* feeling that the *Gerusalemme liberata* could be brought into relationship with Milton's poem only in very limited ways. In such judgments, Milton, despite his theoretical acceptance of all the Renaissance commonplaces about epic, went very much his own way in practice. And that path somehow ran closer to the ancient sources than to

125

the contemporary varieties of tradition. Though Spenserian scholarship has conventionally looked to both Tasso and Ariosto as
significant predecessors for the *Faerie Queene*, scholarship on
Paradise Lost, Spenser's major heir in the inward turning of epic,
has found Tasso to be of local, rather than general importance.[1]

But perceiving Tasso as a crucial poet in the epic drive inward
suggests large relationships and lines of analogy with *Paradise
Lost*. Such a re-evaluation of the *Gerusalemme liberata* increases
its importance as a predecessor of *Paradise Lost*, and revises the
current notion that Milton's poem represents a total "bouleversement" of the heroic tradition. Tasso's poem served not only as a
mine of phrases and motifs, but as a model for Christian epic of
crucial significance because its themes, structure and language provide a closer analogy to *Paradise Lost* than literary historians have
discerned.

The Revaluation of the Heroic

Milton saw himself as writing within an admired tradition inherited from ancient culture. But like Tasso, he assumes a highly
critical posture toward that culture and the values of its greatest
literature. In the very process of imitating the large effects of the
classical poems—elevation of tone, extra-ordinary diction, concentration on idealized figures expressing a vision of nobility—he
fundamentally rejects the classical heroic, and claims superiority
for his own Christian alternative. The language of the classical
heroic world undergoes a profound metamorphosis in his re-
creation of it.

Milton imitates ancient heroic language so successfully that
readers continually mistake the figure around whom that language
centers for the "hero" of the poem. And Satan *is* the ancient hero
par excellence.[2] Through the figure of the "father of lies," Milton
mounts a radical critique of the classical heroic. We hear in Satan
the familiar voice of pride, integrity to an individual sense of
honor, and determined will to remain in a chosen course, however
fated or wrong. With perfect decorum the narrator, shortly after
the first scene in Hell, deliberately recalls classical descriptions of
armies and compares the marching demons to "heroes old":

> . . . anon they move
> In perfect phalanx to the Dorian mood

Of flutes and soft recorders; such as raised
To highth of noblest temper heroes old.

(Paradise Lost I, 549–52)

Milton describes them as the epitome of all that heroic poetry has most admired. They breathe "deliberate valour"; they are "firm and unmoved"; (I, 554) and they present a "horrid front / of dreadful length and dazzling arms, in guise / of warriors old . . ." (I, 563–65). "Their mighty chief" responds to this sight of his "battalion . . . Their visages and stature as of gods" (I, 570), after they have just been identified at length with the gods of the ancient world, who were "devils adored as deities" (I, 365–520): "And now his heart / Distends with pride, and hardening in his strength / Glories" (I, 571–73). This response characterizes the Archfiend as a genuine hero of the ancient mold. Milton further reinforces this association by the famous simile that follows, in which Satan's army surpasses all the armed might celebrated in ancient epic and "what resounds / In fable or romance."[3]

From the outset the poet associates the traditional language, characters and events of epic tradition with the works of Satan. Satan expresses the values of ancient heroic literature, and the narrative of his rebellion against God and subsequent "ruin" embodies traditional epic subject matter within *Paradise Lost*. Raphael relates to Adam the "high matter" of the "exploits / of warring spirits" with the full complement of epic conventions, epithets, oratory, descriptions of weapons, and traditional images. Yet within that context the narrator constantly reminds us that this warfare is mere "force" and "violence" (VI, 35, 41), made necessary by the rebellious angels' sin. He presents the figure of Abdiel to teach us a better heroism:

> . . . well hast thou fought
> The better fight, who single hast maintained
> Against revolted multitudes the cause
> Of truth, in word mightier than they in arms;
> And for the testimony of truth hast borne
> Universal reproach, far worse to bear
> Than violence. . . .
>
> (VI, 29–35

In contrast, he condemns the dispute of arms as "brutish and foul" (VI, 124). But he describes that contest in a language overwhelmingly reminiscent of epic tradition. In the configuration of Satan

and the fallen angels and in the entire recounting of the war in
heaven, Milton simultaneously imitates and radically criticizes the
classical heroic tradition.

Like every other aspect of man's fallen condition, war is the
invention of Satan. We come to understand that the war in heaven
provides both source and archetype for the "slaughter and gigantic
deeds," the "violence, . . . oppression, and sword-law" (XI, 659,
672) that characterize human history, as Michael reveals it to the
penitent Adam. The war in heaven prepares us for the radical
rejection of warriors and the deeds of war as embodiments of
"heroic virtue," in the famous declaration of a new subject matter
for "heroic song" in the prologue to Book IX. The narrator repeats
the vocabulary of the conventional heroic code in a context of
explicit condemnation in Book XI, as Adam is taught the
paradoxes and deceptions of fallen history: the evil in "worldly
strong and worldly wise" and "that suffering for truth's sake / Is
fortitude to highest victory" (XII, 569–70). The old ideas of "fortitude" and "victory" emerge as part of man's sin-inspired admiration for "violence" and "brutishness."

> For in those days might only shall be admired,
> And valour and heroic virtue called;
> To overcome in battle, and subdue
> Nations, and bring home spoils with infinite
> Manslaughter, shall be held the highest pitch
> Of human glory; and for glory done,
> Of triumph, to be styled great conquerors,
> Patrons of mankind, gods, and sons of gods,
> Destroyers rightlier called and plagues of men.
> Thus fame shall be achieved, renown on earth,
> And what most merits fame in silence hid.
>
> (XI, 689–99)

In Milton's view, this ancient "virtue" is essentially corrupt.
Those whom he shows "in acts of prowess eminent / And great
exploits" are "of true virtue void" and "having spilt much blood,
and done much waste / Subduing nations, and achieved thereby /
Fame in the world, high titles, and rich prey, / Shall change their
course to pleasure, ease, and sloth, / Surfeit, and lust . . ." (XI,
789–95). He then provides a summary of the total depravity arising
from a world of constant war, in which all are conquerors or
conquered. The characteristic piling up of abstract, generalized
terms achieves the effect of a "root-and-branch" condemnation of

the whole range of values and activities associated with the traditional heroic ideal. By talking about warfare in the language traditionally used to describe and evaluate it, he also condemns the
literature that saw "glory, valour, heroic virtue, triumph, prowess,
and great exploits" in the "massacre . . . of their brethren" begun
with "the sin of him who slew / His brother" (XI, 678). He denies
the value of that literature as it creates "fame" and "renown on
earth" for these "Death's ministers."

Milton's panorama of history explicitly reevaluates the ancient
heroic code, naming the abstract concepts embodied in it. He
forces us to see that men throughout the flux of temporal history
reenact the sins originated by Satan and the fallen angels. Satan, the
archetype of the hero who talked of "glory" and "triumph," was in
actuality a "destroyer," and the war in heaven the original of the
historic conflicts celebrated in other epics. Milton identifies the
classical heroic ideal with the principle of evil through the language
surrounding Satan in the early books and through the re-creation
of a traditional epic narrative in Raphael's recounting of the war in
heaven.[4]

This radical critique of the conventional idea of the heroic has
been described as a "Copernican Revolution" in epic tradition, "a
literary *renversement* that overthrows and displaces its predecessors."[5] But there is a striking predecessor of Milton's technique for
challenging epic formulae and the literary prototypes in which
they were embodied: *La Gerusalemme liberata.*[6] In the background of Milton's "Rebel Angels," stands the whole re-creation
of the classical ethic in the great pagan warriors, and the resulting
complexity of attitude toward that ethic in Tasso's poem. When
we hear Satan vowing eternal enmity ("What though the field be
lost? / All is not lost; the unconquerable will, / And study of
revenge, immortal hate, / And courage never to submit or yield,"
I, 105–8), we can recognize the voice of fierce pride and indomitable will embodied by Tasso in Argante and Solimano ("Non cedo
io, no; fia con memoria eterna / De le mie offese eterno anco il mio
sdegno," IX, 99). The Archfiend summoning his demons to a
council with "Princes, potentates, / Warriors" (I, 315) recalls Tasso's Plutone exhorting his "Tartarei numi" to rekindle "Gli spirti
. . . di quel valor primiero" (IV, 9, 15).

Milton builds on Tasso's example in his technique for condemning the traditional idea of the heroic. His "innovation on the heroic
tradition," therefore, *was* "an innovation *within* the tradition."[7]
As a result of Tasso's precedent Milton can maintain a sense of

continuity with valued literary qualities while accomplishing a radical reorientation of moral values. *Paradise Lost* is very much analogous to the *Gerusalemme* in the attitudes expressed toward the classical past. But because Tasso, the model of the epic poet ranked with Homer and Virgil, did precede him in this kind of critique, Milton can forge links to a continuing tradition, while he pushes his criticism of ancient values to a much more extreme position than had ever before been taken. As in Tasso these classical parallels also achieve positive ends. In the very act of damning epic conventions, Milton places his own poem within the tradition, by imitating the expressive devices of older heroic literature.

In addition, Milton builds up the parallels between the fall of the rebel angels and the fall of man through repeated images, phrases, allusions, and through the objective relationship of cause and effect (the fall of Satan is the necessary precondition for the creation and the fall of man).[8] Milton offers the fall of the angels as the conventional epic conflict. He makes the war in heaven the traditional battle of classical heroes, specifically suggesting characteristics of most of the famous literary heroes at various points in the portrayal of Satan. In constructing analogies between man's fall and the angelic rebellion, he identifies the human "breach disloyal" with events that he has characterized as heroic. He uses heroic language to describe conventionally valued events and characters while teaching us to see their true degradation, thereby condemning traditional attitudes and language. But in summoning traditional associations to such language he also confers dignity, authority, "magnificence, " on those events. The parallel between the angelic fall and the human, the analogy of the war in heaven to the psychological conflict in Adam and Eve, contributes to the effect of grandeur and tragic stature in the narrative of "man's first disobedience." Adam's fall, like Satan's, becomes "high matter."

Milton, like Tasso, uses his re-creation and simultaneous condemnation of the traditional heroic to incorporate the authority associated with it into a new vision of what constitutes the heroic in human life. Here too Milton both continues in the direction suggested by Tasso and moves to a radical end point. Milton develops the potentiality in the *Gerusalemme* for a psychological and spiritual idea of the heroic as a foundation for an epic of the inner life of the Christian conscience. The "argument," which he declares is "more heroic" than the wars and "tinsel trappings" of his predecessors, is a wholly moral conflict. "That which justly gives heroic name / To person or to poem" (IX, 13–41) is doing battle within the soul, with defeat or victory defined only in spiritual terms.

Milton develops further than Tasso an awareness of the problematic nature of the epic poet's need to accommodate an admired tradition, which he sees as the model for beauty and order in artistic creation, but whose ethical and spiritual foundation he must reject. His vision of a redeemed heroic demands not merely the transformation of traditional martial subject matter into a holy war, which can serve as the catalyst and symbol of the inner conflicts of the Christian soul. He insists on an epic narrative about the spiritual realities themselves. He "transubstantiates"[9] the traditional epic themes by embodying the holy war of heaven and hell directly, and making it the literal as well as figurative theme of the poem.

He also pushes Tasso's sense of the cosmic inclusiveness of epic treatment to the point of literally including the entire universe in the world of his poem, and incorporating all of time, from the eternity before the creation to the eternity after the Last Judgment, into the entwined cycles of the narrative. He can nevertheless maintain the necessary specificity of a narrative about particular events involving specific people at one time, because he chose for epic treatment the one event that he could see as both origin and archetype of all other events. The poem reveals to us the pattern of temptation, sin, fall, and redemption in all human experience, unifying the varieties and paradoxes of history, linking inseparably the natural and supernatural. Human and divine events are inextricably involved in a necessary cycle of events that demonstrate repeatedly the mercy and power of God: "That all this good of evil shall produce, / And evil turn to good; more wonderful / Than that which by creation first brought forth / Light out of darkness!" (XII, 470–73).

Yet this cosmic inclusiveness is centered on the drama of the individual soul in its constant confrontation between rebellious sin and obedient repentance through "love with fear" for "the only God" (XII, 562). The epic is literally universal in the scope of the narrative itself, and figuratively in its representation of a constant pattern in experience. Because he chose a "favola" about spiritual entities which nevertheless carried the validity of specific, sensory experience, Milton could create genuine epic that is wholly moral and psychological in subject and meaning. He completely transmutes our understanding of what constitutes heroic action to spiritual conflict. He defines the idea of the heroic purely in terms of the interior life.

The imitation of traditional epic confers authority and grandeur on the new heroic, so that the poem arouses the traditional responses of "meraviglia" and love of excellence in relation to wholly inward defeats and victories. As a result, heroic poetry itself is redeemed, because language and form based in tradition have become the vehicle for a Christian vision of heroic virtue and the human ideal. By his success in accommodating the strain of the old against the new heroism, creating large analogies between traditional epic grandeur and the poetry of Christian life, the poet "saves" the epic as a valued form.

The Language of Figurative Narration

To achieve such ends, Milton exploits a uniquely appropriate language of figurative narration. Though it clearly resembles his earlier poetic language in many ways, its most striking qualities are designed for the demands of an epic narration that must order literally everything—time and eternity, nature and supernature, the visible and the invisible. In comparison to his predecessors including Tasso, Milton is radical in the Latin sense. He achieves truth and authority by returning to the source of all experience, "the root of all our woe." The "heavenly muse" inspires him with a vision of events that are unquestionably valid because his readers have heard them before in God's words. And these events lie at the root of all other stories. In Milton's hands, the story of the fall ultimately encompasses all of natural and supernatural history. He constructs the characters and events of his epic as the archetypes of all later characters and events. The need for a true narrative at the foundation of a heroic poem led him to Scripture. He chose the one Scriptural narration that could convincingly include the entire Christian scheme, because of the traditional version of universal history in hexameral literature. By his radical return to the root of all other stories he cuts away the particularity of any one human experience. He engages the most basic issues. But in his treatment they also become the most general, because the language of the "illumined" blind bard, the narrator of the vision,[10] includes all subsequent particularities. He sees and makes us see both the temporal and conceptual connections between these original events and all other events in history. In the process, he finds it necessary to move much farther in the direction of a heroic of the inner life than any other creator of epic.

In the search for unity of vision that could, nevertheless, encompass the variety and contradiction of history, Milton created a narrative style that could support with equal validity both the demands of the story and the moral and spiritual meaning that he sought to convey. Milton saw the narrator of *Paradise Lost* as both "the singer of tales" and as prophet, revealing the truths of man's spiritual history and present state.

Several critics have shown the completeness and complexity with which Milton achieved a poem in which "image and meaning are one."[11] He accomplishes this by his use of "true" myth, i.e., a myth from Scripture. The events of such a story are particular. They occurred in one place and time. And yet they are universal. The fall of man resonates as the beginning and explanation for all subsequent historical experience. Metaphorically, it stands for constantly recurring events in the spiritual life of all men. By going back to what a believing Christian of the seventeenth century saw as the source for all other myths, indeed for all other stories, Milton endowed the literal appearances of his poem with a validity that no other subject matter could provide.[12]

A concern for the truth of his poem, analogous to Tasso's, lies at the foundation of Milton's drive to this extreme point. But he goes further than Tasso, who sought a conviction of truth in the audience through the historical reliability of major events and through the verisimilitude of his presentation. Milton creates instead the persona of a narrator who can translate "things invisible to mortal sight," and present events and states impossible for fallen man to experience; yet these events include and explain fallen history.

In order to re-create in verse events that are at once particular and universal, Milton invents a language that refers simultaneously to physical, literal events and places and to inner states or qualities. In this capacity to express both concrete and abstract meanings, his language, like that of Scripture, gives life to unique historical actions and to perennial conditions of the psyche.[13] The "spatial" quality of the poem provides a comprehensive example of this kind of language, and it is one particularly interesting to the reader approaching *Paradise Lost* from the *Gerusalemme liberata*. In *Paradise Lost*, rising and falling constitute the major movements of its actors. Such upward or downward movements refer to literal changes of place as well as to emotional or moral shifts. Milton's use of language indicating place or direction continually welds together literal and figurative meanings. More generally, "the spiritual forces at work in the action, though they may be invisible to mortal sight, can be given a degree of unseen but physical reality, by being located in the poem's imaginative structure. The construction of a plan in which physical areas had moral meaning . . . [makes] it possible to characterize immaterial forces by telling where they lived and where they went; it is a method unique in Paradise Lost."[14]

In the coherence with which it is used, it is a method unique in *Paradise Lost*. But to the reader of Tasso this method suggests some lines of relationship to its Italian predecessor that would qualify the distinctness with which *Paradise Lost* ought to be set apart from the formal tradition in which it was written. The word "wander" for instance offers, in condensed form, the particular kind of unity Milton achieves in his language. "The word *wander* has almost always a pejorative, or melancholy, connotation in *Paradise Lost*. It is a key word, summarizing the theme of the erring, bewildered human pilgrimage, and its extension into the prelapsarian world with the fallen angels. . . . Not only moral values, but the intellectual values on which they depend, can be objectified in Milton's topography, by the identification of physical and spiritual 'wandering.' *Error* is the linking word."[15]

This feature of Milton's language, the creation of both literal and figurative meanings for places and directions, and particularly the specific example of the word *wander*, suggest a parallel to Tasso's poem. For there also the place, "Jerusalem," the physical movement, "going on Crusade," take on moral meaning. And in the *Gerusalemme*, physical wandering away from the Crusade, away from Jerusalem, is also a moral "fall" into "error." Tasso's use of the verb *errare* seems very much analogous to Milton's use of *wander* in *Paradise Lost*. There is also a striking parallel in the general effort to achieve a conviction of truth in the particular "*favola*" on which the poem is based, while expressing at the same time universal, moral themes related to the interior life. Both poets work toward such a metaphoric language by means as specific as a verb that can signify both physical action and moral meaning, and as general as the traditional spiritual implications attached to a geographical place.

I am suggesting here that we can discern a substantial relationship between some of the most essential and pervasive qualities of Milton's language and some aspects of Tasso's language in the

Gerusalemme. This does not mean that Milton "modeled" his creation of metaphor on Tasso's. Rather, it would indicate that, given the unity of vision and expression Milton sought to achieve, Tasso's poem offered him an admired example of epic in which he could find the potentiality for this idea of a heroic diction. And in the Italian poem such language emerges from a structure built on a respect for classical discipline analogous to his own.

Like Tasso, Milton placed demands on his narrative style derived from the self-conscious position he occupied in the history of epic poetry. This makes Tasso a particularly crucial predecessor in the creation of a language of figurative narration.[16] Clearly there are other essential poems in this regard, on which Milton built and from which he learned both positively and negatively—the *Aeneid*, the *Commedia*, and most immediately, *The Faerie Queene*. In all these poems, for instance, the narrative exploits the potential ambiguity and connotative richness of physical wandering, becoming lost, drifting or being driven "off course." Yet Spenser's poem in particular must be considered especially closely akin to *Paradise Lost* in any account of the ancestry of Milton's decisive turn inward.[17] According to Dryden, Milton called Spenser "his original."[18] And among the significant models for epic, only the *Faerie Queene* is a heroic and figurative narration by an English Protestant poet, seeking to remake epic poetry into a vehicle for moral and psychological experience.

If we examine the ways in which Spenser, in comparison to Tasso or Milton, uses figurative language so that his story tells of the life of the mind, we can see more sharply the distinctive branches of this intricately entwined family tree. In comparison to Spenser, Milton strives for a language that welds into unity radically separate dimensions of experience, while maintaining, in fact, reinforcing, our perception of the division. For the one absolutely fundamental rupture in being, the irrevocable split between unfallen and fallen existence, is the subject and condition of his poem. Every word conveying the quality and meaning of life before history is conditioned by history, Milton's deliberate evocation of the etymological development embedded in English words[19] constantly calls attention to the distinction between "then" and "now" in the immediate perception of meaning as well as in the understanding of larger narrative structures.[20] This existential duality is mirrored in the double demand he places on his language and the narrative it conveys—to be literally and particularly true, but also metaphorical.

Spenser, like Tasso, creates a world in history, though its position in time remains deliberately fluid, thus opening the possibility for action understood to be "in the mind."[21] But Spenser designs his narrative language to begin with division, only to move toward unity, If, as Isabel MacCaffrey has argued convincingly, we must conceive the material or visible referents of Spenser's allegorical language as particulars bodying forth immanifest universals upon which the particulars depend, the *visibilia* of his narrative are logically subordinate to the assumed universals.[22] His language and narrative sequences push us to "see" beyond the *visibilia* and ultimately to discard them ("Graunt me that Sabaoths sight"). He does not work for the effects of literal historicity demanded by both Tasso and Milton, and his language arouses unified, though complex, responses, if we attend to it carefully ("well auis'd," II, xii, 61).[23] Tasso, on the other hand, made a language like Milton's, not only in the stylistic characteristics of "magnificenza" detailed by F. T. Prince, but in the quality of response solicited from the audience. For Tasso, as for Milton, the concern for literal validity, for *"il verosimile,"* aroused the need for a language of figurative narration that could be mimetically reliable. His language tries to create a conviction that its fictive universe accords with experience and at the same time allows for figurative meanings. It tends to invite divided responses, though the sources of division are, of course, quite different from such issues in *Paradise Lost*. Nevertheless, this essential duality in the demands placed on narrative language and in the responses to it makes Tasso's language analogous to Milton's in ways that are particularly illuminating of their problematic relation to their own tradition.

To substantiate such a description of the relationships among the narrative styles of these three poems which re-create classical epic for Christian purposes and turn it inward, I will examine the language of three crucial and characteristic passages,[24] all of them versions of a highly traditional topos in western epic—the garden or earthly paradise. Tasso, Spenser, and Milton all create such gardens and, as is typical of Renaissance as opposed to classical or medieval gardens, use them as settings for crucial temptation scenes.[25] The two English poets, moreover, substantially appropriate the details and actual language of their predecessors' versions. Spenser literally translates passages from Cantos XV and XVI of the *Gerusalemme liberata* (Armida's garden) in the Bower of Bliss episode (*Faerie Queene*, II, xii). Milton echoes both Spenser and Tasso in the description of Eden in Book IV of *Paradise*

Lost.[26] Such close alliances make the resemblances and differences in language particularly suggestive for an understanding of the effects on narrative style of the turn inward of epic and for an evaluation of the importance of Tasso's poem in the history of that inward turn which, furthered by the *Faerie Queene,* culminates in *Paradise Lost.*

Spenser's use of Tasso in the Bower of Bliss episode is especially revealing, because he translates, rather than echoing or otherwise alluding to Tasso's language. C. S. Lewis said that the *Faerie Queene*'s relation to Italian epic is as intimate as fighting in another man's armor.[27] In this episode, however, Spenser not only wears Tasso's armor, but travels the same stretch of forest and fights the same battles. It is the most extensive re-creation of a part of Tasso's poem in an original English work, and yet the translation invites quite different responses.[28]

I begin with sections of this complex imitation of Tasso in Book II—canto xii, stanzas 60–68, modeled on *Gerusalemme liberata* XV, 55–62 (see appendix). Spenser has established the same narrative context here. Guyon, like Tasso's Carlo and Ubaldo, has come to an earthly paradise, conceived as the richly sensual center and epitome of the temptations of this world. His task, and ours with him, is "to see and know and yet abstain," as Milton put it.[29] Milton's phrase is extraordinarily appropriate for both poems, because we experience the temptation here through seeing in all senses of the word. Armida's garden and the Bower of Bliss are constructed primarily as pictures appealing to the senses visually. But heroes and readers are also made to see in the sense of understand both the appeal and danger of the place. In both poems the primarily visual presentation of the gardens as a series of spectacles enacts the subtle combination of involvement with and detachment from the scene, necessary if we are going to understand the experience.

Spenser's narrative strategy demands one shift, however, that becomes crucial to the qualities of language I will examine. He represents these sights as temptations to the central hero. We are constantly made to perceive the effects on Guyon of all this luxury and sexual invitation. Moreover, the journey to the Bower occupies the culminating position in the structure of Book II as a whole. It is the final goal of Guyon's quest. The poet, already using Tasso's language extensively, anticipates this final garden scene in the earlier description of Cymochles in the Bower (II, v, 27–37) and in the smaller-scale *locus amoenus,* Phaedria's island

(II, vi, 11–18, 24–26). Indeed, Spenser's description of the fountain reminds us of the very origin of the quest in canto i, the
fountain of tears, where Guyon first heard about Acrasia and saw
the destructive consequences of her power in the death of Mordant
and Amavia. In Tasso, though the passage through Armida's garden is also essential to the narrative structure, it represents a stage
in the movement of the crusade, not an end point. Moreover,
Tasso constructs a more distant point of view, through peripheral
characters. Because their response to the place is less rich and
interesting to narrator and reader, the narrative provides less inter-
mingling of subjective and objective aspects of the experience.

In Spenser's translation of Tasso's description of the fountain
"in the midst" (II, xii, 60ff.), his language insistently calls attention
to the artifice of the fountain, artifice in the double sense of "made
by art" and "fraudulent." The physical imagery, "a fountaine . . .
of richest substaunce," "the silver flood," "with curious imageree
was ouer-wrought," immediately begins to acquire moral implications which become explicit in the next stanza. The ivy made of
metal is "coloured" (both literally and, figuratively, "disguised")
to look like the natural plant, causing confusion to "that wight"
who does not look "well auis'd." The very act of seeing becomes a
moral act, the discovery of the difference between falsehood and
truth. In such a context the "shapes of naked boyes / Of which
some *seemd* . . . to fly about" with their "wanton toyes," the ivy's
"lasciuious arms," the flowers "which drops of Christall seemd for
wantones to weepe," all carry moral as well as physically descriptive connotations. Reinforced by the implied comparison with the
weeping fountain of canto i,[30] the crystal drops of these "infinit
streames" form part of a description at once more particular and
more evaluative than Tasso's. The Italian model emphasizes simple, natural beauty, conveyed through general evocations of the
pleasance ("verdi sponde," "l'acqua . . . gelida e bruna," "ma
trasparente sì, che non asconde . . . vaghezza alcuna") and through
reproduction by rhyme and assonance of the smooth, lulling, easy
effect of the place. The fountain itself poses the natural temptation
of quenching thirst for the two warriors who are "alquanto affaticati e lassi" after climbing the mountain. Only after the moral
speech by the warriors and, more importantly, after the lavishly
sensual depiction of the "donzellette," the maidens bathing in the
fountain, might one perceive the potential danger in the fountain's
invitation to "bathe their dry lips."

Our awareness of Spenser's greater emphasis on moral as well as physical perception here increases because of his two preceding stanzas.

> There the most daintie Paradise on ground,
>   It selfe doth offer to his sober eye,
>   In which all pleasures plenteously abound,
>   And none does others happinesse enuye:
>   The painted flowres, the trees vpshooting hye,
>   The dales for shade, the hilles for breathing space,
>   The trembling groues, the Christall running by;
>   And that, which all faire workes doth most aggrace,
> The art, which all that wrought, appeared in no place.
>
> One would haue thought, (so cunningly, the rude,
>   And scorned parts were mingled with the fine,)
>   That nature had for wantonesse ensude
>   Art, and that Art at nature did repine;
>   So striuing each th'other to undermine;
>   Each did the others worke more beautifie;
>   So diff'ring both in willes, agreed in fine:
>   So all agreed, through sweete diuersitie,
> This Gardin to adorne with all varietie.
>
> (II, xii, 58–59)

They represent his version of the motif, traditional to such a "dainty paradise on ground," of art vying with nature. Stanza 59 translates Tasso's lines on the same theme.

> Stimi (sì misto il culto è co'l negletto)
> Sol naturali e gli ornamenti e i siti.
> Di natura arte par, che per diletto
> L'imitatrice sua scherzando imìti.
>
> (XVI, 10)

> One would think (so mixed is the cultivated with the wild)
> The site and its embellishments totally natural.
> Art seems nature, which for pleasure
> Plays at imitating her imitator.

But Spenser dwells on the total blurring of the boundaries between art and nature in morally ambiguous language, whereas Tasso suggests a playfulness and aesthetic delight in the baroque confusion of illusion and reality. Also, Spenser has shifted the stanza to occur much earlier in the description of the earthly paradise, so that the deceptive merging of art and nature stands like the frontispiece or portal to the Bower rather than along the way. We are, therefore, influenced much earlier by the moral implications of a confusion between illusion and reality. Although critics since C. S. Lewis have noticed this emphasis on the moral implications of artifice in the Bower, the comparison with Tasso shows how persistently and subtly Spenser writes so that the meaning and evaluation of what we see are perceived simultaneously with the visual image.

Tasso's simpler, more straightforward images of natural elements evoke physical responses first in the temporal sequence of reading or hearing. The moral language is juxtaposed, rather than implied in the descriptive language itself. Though in Canto XV, 57, he exploits the fact that *rio* can mean both "a stream" and "evil," this occurs in a separate stanza devoted to the heroes' deliberate controlled response, not in the description itself. This narrative sequence invites us to divide our responses to the sensually appealing spectacle of the beautiful landscape and the sexually exciting "damsels" from the rational judgment of the scene as dangerous temptation. The musicality and the sensual appeal of the poetry itself increase the impact of the scene in both Spenser's and Tasso's versions.[31] But in the *Gerusalemme liberata,* the *narrator* breaks into exclamations expressing sympathetic involvement with the pleasures of the place. In stanza 61, the repetition of "lor tolto," "loro tolse" calls special attention to the sense of loss experienced by the narrator. As readers, we are encouraged to respond to the appeal of the scene and then to judge.

Spenser prevents such ambivalence in response by structuring the narrative with a unified perspective. We see through Guyon's eyes and are alerted to the effects of these sights on his psyche. In stanza 63 (lines 5–9), for instance, he adapts Tasso's XV, 58. But instead of the objective presentation of the "due donzellette garrule," he filters the images through the hero's perceiving eye ("Two naked Damzelles he therein espyde"), and makes that eye a representative consciousness ("ne car'd to hyde/Their dainty parts from vew of *any, which* them eyde"). Spenser insists particularly on Guyon's looking in his beautiful translation, in stanza 65, of Tasso's equally lovely simile (XV, 60) for the maiden as "la dea d'amore." Though, in his first six lines, he translates almost literally, he uses the last three lines, not for Tasso's continued description of the maiden's actions, but for Guyon's responses, both physical and emotional. And the inner dimension receives the emphasis of its position as the last line of the stanza.

This change in point of view provides a clue to the different quality of the sexuality in the Bower of Bliss. If we compare the stanzas devoted to the sexual teasing of these bathing girls (*Gerusalemme liberata* XV, 58–59 and *Faerie Queene* II, xii, 63–64), we find in Tasso again an objective description by the narrator, designed to present direct sensual appeal (later intensified by the narrator's interjections in stanza 61). Spenser presents his naked damsels through Guyon's eyes, and emphasizes the hero's intense, lustful looking. His verbs, *eyd, espyde,* take on the connotation of a sexual leer, a voyeuristic intensity confirmed by the characterization of his eyes as "greedy eyes." This combines with a muscular tension in the description of the damsels themselves who "contend and wrestle wantonly," joining in a physical intimacy that suggests both sex and aggression. When, in stanza 64, we hear of "sweet spoiles" revealed to "greedy eyes" with connotations from warfare, the looking becomes a kind of rape.

Both Guyon's responses and the women's sexual teasing create an atmosphere of perversion, of corrupted sensuality, amplified later on at the center of the Bower in the scene of Acrasia with Verdant. By this presentation, Spenser makes us feel simultaneously both the attraction and the essential destructiveness of this scene. At the very moment of perception through Guyon's eyes, it arouses a perverted, corrupting sexual response. Spenser, very powerfully, insures that the moral judgment of the sights is implicit and intricately involved in our experiencing of them. The response, though complex, is unified. Language and narrative technique provide clarity about the moral and psychological value of this false paradise. When Spenser wants to explore the nature of healthy and creative physical love, he makes another, separate, imagined place, the Garden of Adonis. In that paradise, a much more philosophical language and a narrative sequence based on conceptual relationships give tangible expression to the positive implications of human sexuality. But in this temptation scene, where he is interested in uncontrolled, undisciplined sensuality, he presents an excessive, sterile sexuality, inherently corrupt and corrupting. He organizes his language so as to make the appeal of the place a matter of surfaces, alerting us to its deceptive nature by his (here) critical emphasis on artifice and the blurring of illusion and reality.

In all of Spenser's borrowings from Tasso, he changes the language and/or context so as to give greater weight to the inward

dimension of experience and to increase the clarity of moral judgments. Perhaps the emblematic example would be Spenser's use of
the famous *carpe diem* song at the center of the Bower.

> Vola, fra gli altri, un che le piume ha sparte
> Di color vari, ed ha purpureo il rostro;
> E lingua snoda in guisa larga, e parte
> La voce sì, ch'assembra il sermon nostro.
> Questi ivi allor continovò con arte
> Tanta il parlar, che fu mirabil mostro.
> Tacquero gli altri ad ascoltarlo intenti;
> E fermaro i susurri in aria i venti.
>
> —Deh mira, egli cantò, spuntar la rosa
> Dal verde suo modesta e virginella,
> Che mezzo aperta ancora, e mezzo ascosa,
> Quanto si mostra men, tanto è più bella.
> Ecco poi nudo il sen già baldanzosa
> Dispiega: ecco poi langue, e non par quella;
> Quella non par, che desïata inanti
> Fu da mille donzelle e mille amanti.
>
> Così trapassa al trapassar d'un giorno
> De la vita mortale il fiore e'l verde;
> Né, perché faccia in dietro april ritorno,
> Si rinfiora ella mai, né si rinverde.
> Cogliam la rosa in su'l mattino adorno
> Di questo dí, che tosto il seren perde;
> Cogliam d'amor la rosa: amiamo or quando
> Esser si puote rïamato amando.—

(XVI, 13–15)

There flies among the others one with feathers mixed
in various colors and purple bill;
its tongue sounds far and wide and makes
its voice resemble our speech.
There this bird continued artfully
to talk so much that it was a wondrous prodigy.
The others fell silent, intent on listening to it;
and the breezes ceased their murmurings.

Oh behold, he sang, the rose springing forth
from her green bud, modest and virginal,
so that still half hidden, half revealed,
the less is shown, the more beautiful she is.
Behold then, already daring, her naked breast

she unfolds: behold then she languishes and no longer appears the
   same,
no longer appears that same one, desired before
by a thousand maidens, a thousand lovers.

So passes in the passing of a day
of mortal life the flower and the bud;
nor, though April may return again,
does she / it flower again or again show green her bud.
Gather the rose in the lovely morning
of this day, which soon loses its brightness;
gather the rose of love: let us love now when
we can loving be loved.—

The whiles some one did chaunt this louely lay;
  Ah see, who so faire thing doest faine to see,
  In springing flowre the image of thy day;
  Ah see the Virgin Rose, how sweetly shee
  Doth first peepe forth with bashfull modestee,
  That fairer seemes the lesse ye see her may;
  Lo see soone after, how more bold and free
  Her bared bosome she doth broad display;
Loe see soone after, how she fades, and falles away.

So passeth, in the passing of a day,
  Of mortall life the leafe, the bud, the flowre,
  Ne more doth flourish after first decay.
  That earst was sought to decke both bed and bowre,
  Of many a Ladie, and many a Paramowre:
  Gather therefore the Rose, whilest yet is prime,
  For soone comes age, that will her pride deflowre:
  Gather the Rose of loue, whilest yet is time,
Whilest louing thou mayst loued be with equall crime.

(II, xii, 74–75)

In the first place, Spenser has shifted the order of the stanzas in
which the song occurs. In Tasso, the song is the culmination of a
luxuriant description. He gives the singer physical presence with a
detailed splendor of color and sound. The song itself, musical,
poignant in its melancholy evocation of transient beauty, merges
with the harmonious landscape in which we are allowed to dwell
for many stanzas, until we are brought up short by the moral
perspective of the two observing warriors and by the sight of the
corrupted hero, Rinaldo. Spenser leaves the singer unspecified and
undescribed, and we therefore concentrate more firmly on the

content of the song. Moreover, we hear the song *after* we have
seen Acrasia and Verdant "molten into lust and pleasure lewd."
We cannot hear the song as simply beautiful. It becomes immediately a dangerous beauty. The advice to gather the rose has to
be felt as an unequivocal invitation to sin. Spenser's quite striking
changes in the language are congruent. In the song itself, he asks us
to perceive the rose as an "image," a way of talking about time,
before it is given any physical reality. He then follows Tasso rather
closely until the last line of the second stanza. There the clear
moral judgment of such love receives all the emphasis of a full stop.

Spenser's poetry works for a unified moral and psychological
response. In comparable passages, Tasso's is a poetry expressing,
in fact taking its life from, division. Tasso offers no other context
for sexuality. The kinds of sensual pleasures experienced in Armida's garden with their evil consequences represent the only possible sensual pleasures in Tasso's fictive world, so they must be
judged and abandoned. He expresses equally powerfully the enormous appeal of the false paradise and his moral judgment on it, but
by means of juxtaposition. His language reveals the moral and
psychological dimensions of the scenes it describes less immediately than Spenser's. Even in constructing this imagined
place, whose historical "reality" consists of previous literary embodiments, he strives for an effect of literal validity through geographical and descriptive detail and through the theme of "magic"
reproducing nature.[32] Spenser's version gives greater weight to the
internal dimensions of experience. His language continually works
to transform the tangible world into a landscape of the mind.

Milton's incorporation of the language of these false paradises
into his description of the true paradise reveals the division pervasive in his language of figurative narration. The fallen language of
our ambiguous, historically changing experience must be
"translated" to produce images of an unfallen world. Yet that innocent and perfect existence must be comprehensibly shown to be
capable of change and loss. To that end, we find Milton risking
self-destruction by alluding to the Renaissance gardens of temptation and illusion as well as to the literature on Eden itself.[33] When
he describes the "prospect" given to "our general sire" as "a circl-
ing row/Of goodliest trees loaden with fairest fruit,/Blossoms
and fruits at once of golden hue/Appeared, with gay enamelled
colours mixed" (IV, 146–149), we hear in the generality of Milton's language the suggestion that this place sums up and is the
model for both the dangerous fertility of Tasso's garden[34] and the

benign natural order embodied in Spenser's Garden of Adonis: "There is continuall spring, and haruest there/Continuall, both meeting at one tyme:/For both the boughes doe laughing blossomes beare,/And with fresh colours decke the wanton Prime,/And eke attonce the heauy trees they clime,/Which seeme to labour vnder their fruites lode" (III, vi, 42).

More daringly, he evokes Tasso's garden at the very center of Eden.

> Another side, umbrageous grots and caves
> Of cool recess, o'er which the mantling vine
> Lays forth her purple grape, and gently creeps
> Luxuriant; mean while murmuring waters fall
> Down the slope hills, dispersed, or in a lake,
> That to the fringed bank with myrtle crowned,
> Her crystal mirror holds, unite their streams.
> The birds their choir apply; airs, vernal airs,
> Breathing the smell of field and grove, attune
> The trembling leaves, while universal Pan
> Knit with the Graces and the Hours in dance
> Led on the eternal spring.
>
> (IV, 257–68)

As Fowler notes, the particular combination of *locus amoenus* motifs here is traditional to gardens of Venus, and he appropriately cites both *Gerusalemme Liberata* XVI, 12 and *Faerie Queene* II, xii, 70ff. In both predecessors, the imitation in the poetry itself of a musical harmony derived from bird song, trembling leaves, and murmuring waters strikes the ear. But Milton insists that we hear Tasso's as the dominant voice. In line 260, a long period comes to a pause on a syntactic inversion which causes the potentially ambiguous adjective *Luxuriant* to spring out in bold relief ("o'er which the mantling vine/Lays forth her purple grape, and gently creeps/Luxuriant"). This mirrors exactly the emphasis achieved by Tasso in XVI, 11 where he begins a new clause in the precise middle of his stanza with a syntactic inversion bringing *Lussureggiante* into similar focus ("Lussureggiante serpe alto e germoglia/La tòrta vite . . ." Lxuxuriant creeps high and sprouts the twining vine).[35] In these lines the choir of birds and vernal airs that "attune/The trembling leaves" not only echo the harmonies of Armida's garden, but also one of Tasso's most famous love lyrics set to music by Monteverdi, "Ecco mormorar l'onde e tremolar le fronde."[36]

Eve herself is involved in such suggestions from our first sight of her "in naked majesty" (IV, 290). Like Tasso's maidens, she wears her hair "as a veil down to the slender waist" (IV, 304; *Gerusalemme liberata* XV, 61, 59). The allusion is reinforced by the brief simile, "but in wanton ringlets waved / As the vine curls her tendrils" (IV, 306–7), suggesting prelapsarian harmony between her human and surrounding natural bodies ("the mantling vine," IV, 258; cf. Tasso's description of the hair as "un aureo manto" [a golden mantle], XV, 61), but also beginning the barest hint of her association with places of temptation and sin. If this light touch remains subdued here, it becomes the dominant note a few lines later when Milton explicitly contrasts this innocent nakedness with subsequent sophistication and false modesty in terms designed to call to mind the most famous lines in Tasso's pastoral play, *Aminta*,[37] where the golden age is that time when "honour dishonourable" (IV, 314) had not yet troubled "le liete dolcezze de l'amoroso gregge" (the gay sweets of the flock of lovers, Act I, lines 676–77).[38]

Milton deliberately constructs his large image of innocence and natural virtue, the garden with a pair of lovers, from pieces of imagery taken from the tradition of false paradises, where woman's beauty is the central deceptive attraction to sin and loss of selfhood. He offers, by means of language whose connotative history calls forth moral judgment ("wanton," "luxuriant," "veil," "creeps") the possibility of an imaginative recapturing of its prelapsarian integrity, when such ambiguity did not exist and was unnecessary.[39] But the insistence with which he recalls the fallen meanings of such language and the fallen contexts of these images, by echoing repeatedly the most powerful literary versions of them, insures that connotations created by history (including literary history) remain tensely poised, ready to expand into double meaning, moral and psychological suggestiveness divided from the original concrete referents.

The premonitory narrative techniques through which Milton achieves temporal coherence also unpack these embedded suggestions in the images of innocence. Almost immediately after the narrator details the physical and emotional purity of naked beauty before the Fall, for instance (lines 289–312), he reminds us of what has since happened to our perception of the unclothed human body. The harmony of humans and animals exists for twelve lines, but the first clause is interrupted, in the center of a line, for a dramatically sharp, quick summary of the antithetical state we know so well ("About them frisking played/All beasts of the earth, since wild . . ." IV, 341). And though this is a world of perfect innocence, the serpent is already "sly," and "of his fatal guile/Gave proof unheeded" (IV, 347, 349).

The entire description of Eden proceeds through such ironic loops into subsequent, contrasting states of sin, conflict, and pain. Temporal narrative sequence embodies the pattern of experience incarnated in the myth. We are never allowed to dwell for long in the prelapsarian vision without proleptic hints, anticipatory shadows, just as in history a short sojourn in Eden is followed by "all our woe."[40] But paradise never really exists unshadowed in this narrative. The narrator's descriptive language impresses on us the possibility of an integral language in which words solidify in their original, concrete meanings, without the separate moral or psychological connotations since developed through our experience of sin.[41] But premonition and ironic knowledge pervade the linguistic images he chooses to present the unfallen world, so that in making us "see" the invisible state of innocence he both declares its difference from what we know and suggests that its perfection includes the possibility of a fall. The narrative context only reinforces hints of vulnerability, even fragility. This portrait of the enclosed garden is, after all, itself enclosed by two soliloquies from the agent of the desecration that is to come. Indeed, as the narrator reminds us at each stage of closer focus on the garden, we see all this through the eyes of Satan. We never see Eden without the potentiality for destruction, ". . . and next to life/Our death the tree of knowledge grew fast by . . ." (IV, 221).

The risks in using a language associated with temptation and sin for the innocent love and beauty in Eden include the possibility that innocence has no viable means of expression. What Milton actually achieves is a moment of poise when an integral language, denoting a perfect pleasance and perfect love reveals, yet controls, connotative "levels" of meaning created by history. The fallen narrator, striving to re-create the unfallen in ways that can be comprehensible to his fallen audience, calls attention to the mediation necessary to convey his vision. Language must be "translated" self-consciously, so that we hear, but keep at a distance, the more familiar meanings and associations, just as we do when listening to a partially assimilated "foreign" language in these times "after Babel."

Such division in response is demanded also by the famous epic similes for the garden (IV, 159–71, "As when to them who sail/

Beyond the Cape of Hope . . . though with them better pleased/Than Asmodeus with the fishy fume" and IV, 268–85, "Not that fair field/Of Enna . . ."). Many critics have elucidated the coherent logic of Milton's associations and comparisons, but I am concerned here with the process by which we come to understand that logic and to expand our perception of Eden through those associations. In both cases, the syntactic assertion that connections exist, implied in the conventional phrases indicating simile ("as when," "better pleased than," "Not that fair field . . . might with this Paradise . . . strive; nor"), demands a process of abstraction from each concrete detail in order to make sense of those connections. We must interpret the spiritual significance of the "fishy fume" that Tobit used to drive out Asmodeus and both see the parallel and interpret the spiritual condition of Adam, Eve, and Satan at this moment in Eden. We must select from the Proserpina story the central issue that creates a parallel between the field of Enna and Eden. We are forced to use moral or spiritual categories to make the necessary connections, so that in the process of literally understanding the simile, the "odors," the "field," the place in general are understood as metaphors for a condition of mind or soul. By means of these similes, garnered from subsequent history, the narrative pushes us momentarily into perceiving Eden as it has become in time, a landscape of the mind, a perennial condition or idea of innocence. Again, the very language by which Milton establishes the concrete identity of Eden elicits divided perception. Eden has not yet become a metaphor, but we must be aware of that radical shift, if we are to understand what it is at all.

To elucidate his vision fully, Milton's language, like Tasso's, must accommodate a double perspective, without subordinating one to the other. That tense equipoise—images of the unfallen carved out of fallen language and literary history, spiritual and cosmic reality conveyed by "likening spiritual to corporeal forms" (V, 573)—explodes into double meaning at the Fall. In Book IX, the narrator explicitly invokes the metaphorical meanings of traditional images given concrete validity in this poem. He describes Eve, at the moment of temptation with "storm so nigh" (IX, 433) in a reprise of the evocation of paradise in Book IV (IX, 386–456). But the suggestions of the potential vulnerability of innocence have shifted to insistent statements of imminent fall, and the potentially moral connotations of physical imagery dominate the landscape. "Each flower of slender stalk, whose head though gay/Carnation, purple, azure, or specked with gold, /Hung drooping unsustained, them she upstays / Gently with myrtle band, mindless the while, / Her self, though fairest unsupported flower, / From her best prop so far, and storm so nigh" (IX, 428–33). Here we dwell only momentarily on the physical referents of the images ("Hung drooping unsustained") and move almost immediately to moral or psychological meanings. "Mindless," "Her self . . . unsupported flower," "prop," "storm," etc., work primarily as metaphors, though they continue to refer also to the concrete realities of Eve in the garden. Literary associations are again invoked, but here to their full figurative and associative value. Eve "Herself, though fairest unsupported flower" now explicitly resembles Proserpina about to be raped by death (IV, 269–71, "Proserpine gathering flowers / Her self a fairer flower by gloomy Dis / Was gathered . . ."). Satan "spying" Eve separate sees her "Veiled in a cloud of fragrance, where she stood, / Half spied" (IX 425–26) like Spenser's wanton maidens and even more like the titillating, sense-blurring sight of Tasso's *donzellette*. At this moment when total division from prelapsarian integrity is about to occur, Milton again evokes images that suggest the effects of beauty in the fallen world, not to be exorcised, but to expand in implication through the whole drama of the Fall. Flowers no longer suggest only the gentle beauty of the pleasance, but are more important as figures for Eve's fragility and imminent mortality. Eve is "half spied" because so thickly surrounded with roses, suggesting both Spenser's and Tasso's song of the rose who so quickly "fades and falls away." Adam's garland of flowers, woven as a crown for Eve, whose fall is still unknown to him (IX, 840), becomes the emblem of his fatal recognition of her change and loss ("From his slack hand the garland wreathed for Eve / Down dropped, and all the faded roses shed" IX, 893–94). And in his first speech of horror at her transgression, the flowers have fallen completely to the status of metaphor, whose literal sense derives only from verbal echoes in the poem—"How art thou lost, how on a sudden lost, / Defaced, deflowered, and now to death devote?" (IX, 900–901). Similarly, Eve's veil of hair, which shifted to a partly literal, partly figurative status when Satan sees her veiled in fragrance, has now become the mainly figurative, totally lost veil of innocence ("innocence, that as a veil / Had shadowed them from knowing ill, was gone . . ." IX, 1054–55).

As one consequence of the fall, the poem activates the possibilities for figurative meanings latent in its language for the state of innocence and integrity.[42] Moral and psychological connotations, restrained because not yet appropriate in Book IV, here become equally if not more powerful than concrete meanings for what we hear. Yet the narrative never ceases to assert its literal validity. As he does with many other elements of poetic craftsmanship in the poem—plot structure, literary allusions, epic conventions, traditional epic characters—Milton self-consciously exploits and makes thematically relevant the complexity inherent in using figurative language to tell a story. Like his medieval and Renaissance predecessors in epic, he necessarily invented such a language to make an epic poem in accordance with a Christian understanding of reality. But in the pervasive divisions of response built into his language, he has dealt with the problem of figurative narration in ways that make his poem particularly analogous to Tasso's. Both of these "belated"[43] poets, in their struggle toward a language that will tell "true" stories which also constantly signify beyond the fictive worlds they construct, make more problematic demands on epic narration than Spenser. Spenser subordinates literal, particular meanings to the figurative implications of images or narrative sequences, and consequently his language achieves unified effects. In both the *Gerusalemme liberata* and *Paradise Lost,* the language lives on division.

Epic Tradition

Epic invocations almost inevitably become declarations of allegiance to and divergence from tradition, precisely because they are such conventional moments in epic. In *Paradise Lost,* the poet's self-definition develops through the course of the narrative in recurring invocations, inviting comparison with the *Commedia,* where Dante also expands his poetic identity in renewed prayers for power. To examine such a Miltonic invocation, however, reveals distance in the very moments when he seems to assert his resemblances to Dante.

In the invocation to light at the beginning of Book III (lines 1–55), the narrator's voice shifts from descriptive apostrophe to personal meditation. Beginning with an objective, philosophical delineation of the light he intends to "express" (III, 3), he suggests that the essential history of light (and "God is light" III, 3) consists in the pattern of eternity expressing itself in time through the movement upward from darkness to light ("Before the sun, / Before the heavens thou wert, and at the voice / Of God, as with a

mantle didst invest/The rising world of waters dark and deep,
/Won from the void and formless infinite" III, 8–12). Immediately, however, the apostrophe ceases to expand the names
and lineage of light as an object of praise and shifts attention to the
narrator himself, whose history parallels the movement of light.
He has ventured on a journey down into darkness and now
"taught by the heavenly Muse" (19), rises to "revisit . . . thy
sovereign vital lamp" (22). As light wins a rising world from the
void and formless infinite, the "bolder wing" (13) of the inspired
bard has challenged and mastered "that obscure sojourn" (15) to
sing "of Chaos and eternal Night" (18). Now he has completed the
"hard and rare" (21) enterprise, "to venture down/The dark descent, and up to reascend" (19–20). He claims, then, not simply to
sing about the "Stygian pool" (14), but to have been there, or so it
seems. At this point in the invocation, Milton sounds like Dante.
His narrative is a retelling of what he saw in that dangerous descent.

But the rest of the invocation explores in ever larger terms the
contrast between actual, physical sight and inner vision. Though
the bard "revisits safe" the realm of light and *"feels"* its lamp (22),
light "Revisit'st not these eyes" (23) that "find no dawn" (24). The
apostrophe to light shifts decisively to a meditation on the narrator's total separation from external, "natural" light. From this
perspective, we can notice special qualities in the apparent claim to
traditional visionary authenticity for this poem. The lines suggesting the narrator's participation in the movement from darkness to
light are in the present tense, unlike the narrative itself (and unlike
Dante's statements of his actual presence on the journey he now
recalls). The daring journey "Through utter and through middle
darkness" (16) and back up to the light coexists in time with the
unfolding of the narrative itself, not with the time to which the
narrative refers. In fact, the "flight" is the poem.

The burden of the invocation becomes the inner illumination
which is synonymous with poetry and prophecy. Though the
poet's eyes find no dawn, nevertheless he continually wanders
through those springs, groves and hills which are the Muses' haunt
(27). In those landscapes of the mind, he can perceive a spring as
"clear," a brook as "flowery," a hill as "sunny." The distinction
between sightless eyes and inner vision[44] becomes the distinction
between external, physical experience and poetic creation. Poetry
and prophecy result from figurative journeys in the mind, granted
by the God who transcends nature. In those inner wanderings with

the Muse, sunny hills can be visited "Nightly" (32), for only inner
vision is significant. Though the blind bard with his singing robes
about him is *like* the "wakeful bird" who "Sings darkling" (38–39),
he is a bird that "feed[s] on thoughts" (37). Nature presents him
with "a universal blank" (48), but he can find an even more powerful source of poetry. The invocation rises to prayer for "celestial"
light that shines inward to "irradiate" the "mind through all her
powers" (52). Such divine illumination can create a better nature
("there plant eyes" 53)[45] where vision is not confused or distorted
by mist ("all mist from thence/Purge and disperse" 53–54). The
traditional epic claim to re-create transcendent experience is expressed as prayer for power to "see and tell/Of things invisible to
mortal sight" (54–55). The syntax of the prayer emphasizes simultaneous, rather than sequential actions of the celestial light, by a
series of verbs closely related in meaning, connected by "and"
("shine inward and the mind . . . irradiate," "all mist . . . purge and
disperse"). At the end of a sentence so structured, "see and tell"
also become closely related in meaning and simultaneous. Vision,
we have been taught earlier in the invocation, is the process of
poetic utterance. And the whole invocation has been moving the
content of vision beyond the limitations of nature, even though
divinely created. For the blind bard, surrounded by "ever-during
dark" (45), the object of vision and subject of speech can only be
what is "inward," perceived by all the powers of the mind, "invisible to mortal sight."

    This invocation, like the others in *Paradise Lost*, expresses Mil-
ton's sense of his own poetic nature. Though it is poignantly moving in its autobiographical dimension, it subsumes the individual's
history into the personality of the epic poet. The movement of the
invocation reflects this process of poetic definition. Beginning with
objective description of light in its essence as a cosmic element,
Milton at first claims the relationship to that cosmos traditional for
the epic poet—the seer, the extraordinary traveler into transcendent realms. But neither language nor the movement of subject
matter in these lines permits us to understand this epic poet simply
as a new incarnation of that traditional singer. The invocation
comes to insist on his distinctiveness, his blindness to external
nature and ordinary experience which leaves him open to a better,
because totally inward, illumination. Though he asserts his identity with Homer ("blind Maeonides" III, 35), his language constantly calls attention to the wholly mental realities of his heroic
song. The eyes planted in the mind "see" figuratively, not literally.

Instead of working for the immediacy of Dante's first-person narration, Milton tells his story mediated by the narrative voice of the blind bard. He insists that we cannot "see" immediately and directly. The visionary claim is not, like Dante's, to have "been there" literally, in the flesh ("corruttibile ancora . . . e . . . sensibilmente" [*Inferno* II, 15], still mortal and in his bodily senses), the claim on which he founds his special metaphorical style, and makes it analogous to Scriptural style. Rather, Milton tells us he intends to use the figurative possibilities of poetic language and structure to "make sense" of what he reminds us are "things invisible to mortal sight."[46] The visionary claim is problematic. Rather than marshaling his language to insist on the concrete, tangible reality of its referents, he moves us toward immediate recognition of the universal in the particular, toward interpretation ("Then feed on thoughts").[47]

The whole poem offers itself as, in its essence, interpretation, "an inspired commentary on Scripture."[48] Paradoxically, Milton's radical return to the most fundamental of all stories for his plot allows us to perceive how much the inspired narrator has become a neoclassical "maker." He founds his epic on Scripture, and the absolute truth of Scripture gives it validity. But the first fact about this poem is that it is an interpretation of Scripture. To point to this obvious fact calls attention to the poet's invention. The extent to which the poem is *commentary* on Scripture makes us acutely aware of the difference between this and the biblical version. We experience in almost every line how much history, literature, philosophy, theology the poet brings together, relates, and connects so that a grand design, not apparent in the narrative in *Genesis,* is made visible to us.[49] Though he calls for visionary power, he also makes use of learning on a larger scale and more continuously than any previous poet, accommodating the whole of postlapsarian history and culture to his retelling. He orders all the particulars of subsequent experience into the great explanatory myth, directing our understanding of cause and effect, action and its consequences. The most obvious example, on the stylistic level, of this drive for accommodation is the formal epic simile, where he habitually welds together an enormous cultural range, asserting both connections and a hierarchy of truth or validity within his comparisons ("Not that fair field/Of Enna . . . nor that sweet grove/Of Daphne . . . might with this Paradise/of Eden strive; nor that Nyseian isle . . ." IV, 268–85).

Though the immense weight of structural and linguistic design presses us toward conviction of the poem's truth, we are also constantly aware of the poet's will creating that design. Habitually to call his poem an "argument" as he does, only reinforces that ambiguity. This is no simple retelling of the myth, "true myth" as he understands it to be, but a retelling so as to make sense of it in rational terms ("That to the highth of this great argument / I may assert eternal providence, / And justify the ways of God to men" I, 24–26). He shares with Tasso a particularly intense concern for the truth of the fundamental story on which he erects his poem. Less uneasily than Tasso, he manages to achieve such a conviction of truth, while manifesting at every turn the poet's willful intervention to use the story, to reshape it so that literal events as described *by this poet* constantly refer beyond themselves to make manifest spiritual or psychological experience. Similarly, Tasso sought for a conviction of truth through a historical foundation for his plot. And he too, by using history, calls attention to his own invention, to the connections and design he makes out of the varied materials of his "piccolo mondo." The divergence from verifiable historicity, the wanderings through romantic forests and islands, point up the poet's willful shaping of materials with particular intensity when such clearly imaginative experiences are connected to events and characters derived from chronicles and "official" histories. From this deliberate effort to accommodate a wide-ranging variety (though not as enormous a range as Milton's) emerged the epic of Christian life. The union of the poet's invention with history leads to our perception of historical events as metaphors for the struggles of the militant Christian soul.

In Tasso, the old romantic plot of the quest, merged with the plot of the crusade, is examined critically, and becomes a problem in its literary and moral associations. Though Tasso, like Spenser after him, found in a poetry of chivalric quest a valid metaphor for human life seen as the soul's quest, he makes a poem closer to Milton's in its problematic relation to that metaphor. Traditional individual quest becomes a source of confusion, temptation, even despair. It must be converted to crusade, a Virgilian mission made moral and Christian by the overwhelming figurative associations of the object of that crusade, Jerusalem. For Milton, as for Spenser, individual struggle toward God constitutes the only valid idea of spiritual life. But Milton adopts an even more problematic stance than Tasso's toward traditional romantic images for such individual striving. Like Tasso, he incorporates that traditional subject matter and imagery into his poem, but as self-consciously and more radically examines and overturns its values. The actions of romance (and epic) are both re-created and fundamentally reevaluated in *Paradise Lost* when the narrator seeks images for Satan's activity. In this poem, the heroic quester, the Homeric warrior, the Virgilian discoverer of new lands and founder of empires is "the adversary of God and man." History itself *(gesta)* exists only after the fall as a condition of the lapse from a perfection we can experience, if only obliquely, and whose transformation into the deeds and events of history we therefore feel as loss.

Action is devalued in *Paradise Lost.* The narrator uses the images of heightened action and power that we understand from epic tradition as the "corporal" forms through which to "delineate" the spiritual conflict brought into the world by Satan. The vivid and memorable images of true greatness through which the epic means to teach and move its audience to emulation are images of speech or thought. One thinks of Abdiel whose "better fight" consists of linguistic *gesta,* the courage to speak against Satan and *not to act.* Education for true understanding comes through verbal discourse, the commentaries of Raphael, Michael, and the overarching commentary of the poem itself. The Word, understood ("seen") by the mind, is more trustworthy than deeds observed visually.[50] The traditional commitment of epic to enlarging the significance of human action is strained to the utmost in *Paradise Lost.* Action redefined as activity of the mind and spirit can nevertheless arouse "epic" responses only because of Milton's success in his risky venture of incorporating the language of "high deeds" into a moral universe that continually undermines the values implied in that language.

Milton sacrifices continuing life for the traditional idea of heroic action on the altar of a redeemed poetry of the spirit. Though Tasso's precedent in converting epic structure and language to Christian purposes links *Paradise Lost* to epic tradition in its very subversion of that tradition, the main stream from classical epic ends here.[51] Tasso submits the poetry of romance to the discipline of epic requirements. He allows the individual dream of beauty, the sensual and emotional gratification that arises from indulgence of a solitary, wandering fantasy, to live in his poem only as a stage in the crusade. Moreover, he invests the historical warfare recounted in the poem with moral and psychological dimensions that dominate the representation of literal actions. But traditional epic action remains valid for him. He can redeem the old heroism of effective action in the world, the code of integrity in individual deeds, by integrating it into the communal struggle of holy war. Milton rejects the heroism even of holy war, and ultimately of all physical action. Yet he retains his allegiance to epic as a poetic vehicle for his vision and his redemptive mission. He chose to work in the form in which conventions exercised the most compelling hold on poetic imaginations in the Renaissance, the form most fully defined by past models. He therefore makes the problem of action, traditionally fundamental to epic, unavoidable. Milton grapples with his form at its generic root, and redefines it out of existence. He gives particularly vivid life to the older notion of heroism only to unveil it as temptation. The appeal of individual integrity in action and, for the poet, the representation of such integrity are built into the form Milton insists on using. But he responds to that appeal with an epic that dethrones both the vision of heroism inherited from epic and romance and its representation. Heroic conflict erupts between that very striving for expansion and power that all the models teach us to identify with epic and active acceptance of God's will. Milton confronts his readers with traditional epic at its most problematic. He forces us to face the essential inadequacy, from a Christian perspective, in epic's celebration of action, even when that celebration reveals the inevitable tragedy suffered by its actors. But such recognition splits Renaissance epic poets' uneasy union of heroic images for life in the natural world with Christian insistence on the sole validity of the spirit. Only the unique subject of the Fall allows the poet of *Paradise Lost* to invent a poetry of the mind that still reads like epic because it can subsume traditional epic structures and styles into its revelation of the soul's history. When he found his "higher argument" in the beginning of all stories, Milton marked the end of epic songs in Western Europe.

Notes

Preface

1. "Ad quem Torquati Tassi dialogus extat de Amicitia scriptus; erat enim Tassi amicissimus . . .", etc., *Mansus*, in *The Poems of Milton*, ed. John Carey and Alastair Fowler (London: Longmans, 1968), p. 260. All quotations from Milton's poetry are from this edition.

2. Milton, *The Reason of Church Government*, in *Complete Prose Works of John Milton*, ed. Douglas Bush et al. (New Haven, Conn.: Yale University Press, 1953), vol. 1, p. 813. All quotations from Milton's prose are from this edition.

3. For a detailed discussion of Renaissance reinterpretations of heroic poetry, see Reuben A. Brower, *Hero and Saint: Shakespeare and the Graeco-Roman Heroic Tradition* (New York: Oxford University Press, 1971).

Chapter 1

1. For summary and analysis of the many similar contemporary versions of his ideas see Bernard Weinberg, *A History of Literary Criticism in the Italian Renaissance* (Chicago: University of Chicago Press, 1961); Baxter Hathaway, *Marvels and Commonplaces: Renaissance Literary Criticism* (New York: Random House, 1968) and *The Age of Criticism: The Late Renaissance in Italy* (Ithaca, N.Y.: Cornell University Press, 1962); Joel E. Spingarn, *A History of Literary Criticism in the Renaissance* (New York: Macmillan, 1899; repr. New York: Harcourt, Brace & World, 1963).

2. For detailed discussion of the fusion of Horace and Aristotle in sixteenth-century theory, see Marvin T. Herrick, *The Fusion of Horatian and Aristotelian Literary Criticism, 1531–1555* (Urbana: University of Illinois Press, 1946). For Trissino and Minturno, see Allan Gilbert, *Literary Criticism: Plato to Dryden* (New York: American Book Co., 1940), translations of selections from Giangiorgio Trissino, *Poetica*, 1529 (parts 1–4), 1563 (parts 5 and 6), pp. 210–32, and from Antonio Minturno, *L'Arte Poetica* (1563), pp. 274–303. For full texts see Giovanni Giorgio Trissino, *Tutte le opere* (Verona: Vallarsi, 1729), vol. 2; Antonio Minturno, *L'arte poetica* (Venice: Valvassori, 1563).

3. Horace, *Ars Poetica*, trans. H. R. Fairclough (Cambridge, Mass.: Harvard University Press, 1929).

4. For commentary on these lines in *Ars Poetica*, see C. O. Brink, *Horace on Poetry* (Cambridge: at the University Press, 1971), pp. 352–58, 504. Also, briefly, Steele Commager, *The Odes of Horace* (New Haven, Conn.: Yale University Press, 1962; repr. Bloomington: Indiana University Press, 1967), p. 48.

5. "Saepe temen memorandum inter ludicra memento / Permiscere aliquid breviter, mortalia corda / Quod moveat, tangens humanae commoda vitae, / Quodque olim jubeant natos meminisse parentes." Marco Girolamo Vida, *Ars Poetica*, Book II, 278–81, *Art of Poetry*, trans. Pitt, in *The Art of Poetry: The Poetical Treatises of Horace, Vida and Boileau*, ed. A. S. Cook (Boston: Ginn, 1892), p. 95.

6. Giraldi Cintio (Cinthio), *On Romances*, trans. Henry L. Snuggs (Lexington: University of Kentucky Press, 1968), p. 9. See also G. G. Giraldi Cinzio, *Scritti critici*, ed. Crocetti (Milan: Marzorati, 1973).

7. Bernard Tasso, *Ragionamento della poesia*, in *Lettere di M. Bernardo Tasso* (Padua: Comino, 1733), vol. 2, p. 531; translation in Weinberg, *Literary Criticism*, vol. 1, pp. 282–84.

8. Torquato Tasso, *Discorsi dell'arte poetica e del poema eroico*, ed. Luigi Poma (Bari: Laterza, 1964), p. 67. All quotations from both versions of the *Discorsi* are from this edition. For an English version of the *Discorsi del poema eroico*, see Torquato Tasso, *Discourses on the heroic poem*, trans. I. Samuel and M. Cavalchini (Oxford: Clarendon Press, 1973). Page numbers of subsequent quotations from *Discorsi dell'arte poetica* will be noted in the text.

9. B. Tasso, *Ragionamento della poesia*, p. 526; translation in Weinberg, *Literary Criticism*, vol. 1, p. 282.

10. Plato, *Laws*, Book 2, trans. R. G. Bury (Loeb Classical Library (Cambridge, Mass.: Harvard University Press, 1952), pp. 111–13.

11. Torquato Tasso, *La Gerusalemme liberata*, ed. L. Magugliani (Milan: Rizzoli, 1950). All quotations are from this edition.

12. Torquato Tasso, *Lezione sopra il sonetto: "Questa vita mortal ec. di Monsignor della Casa,"* in *Opere* (Venice: Monti e Compagno, 1736), vol. 6, pp. 453–54.

13. In his definitive edition of the *Discorsi*, Poma argues that the early *Discorsi* were written during Tasso's first period of residence in Padua, 1561–62, when he was involved in a course of lectures given by Sigonio on the *Poetics* of Aristotle, and when he was finishing up the *Rinaldo* and thinking of starting the *Liberata*. He cites as support Tasso in the *Differenze poetiche (Prose diverse*, ed. C. Guasti [Florence: Le Monnier, 1875], 1, p. 435: ". . . in quei *Discorsi* che m'uscirono da le mani essend'io giovinetto, non volli diminuire in alcuna parte la riputazione di quell'autore, ma cercar la verità, e trovar la diritta strada del poetare, da la quale molto hanno traviato i moderni poeti. E benchè io non dovessi, per l'età mia giovenile, farmi guida degli altri, nondimeno, vedendo molte strade e calcate da molti, non sapeva quale eleggere; e mi fermai tra me stesso discorrendo in quel modo che fanno i viandanti ove sogliono dividersi le strade, quando non si avvengono a chi gli mostri la migliore. E scrissi i miei *Discorsi* per ammaestramento di me stesso." As is evident from these statements, the possibility of the somewhat earlier date of composition does not change the intellectual relationship between the *Discorsi* and the *Liberata* assumed in my discussion.

14. See B. T. Sozzi, "La Poetica del Tasso," *Studi Tassiani* 5 (1955), repr. Bergamo: Centro Tassiano (1963): 7–70.

15. For *Parere di Francesco Patrizi in difesa di Lodovico Ariosto* and *Discorso di Torquato Tasso sopra il parere fatto dal signor Francesco Patricio in difesa di Lodovico Ariosto*, see Tasso, *Opere* (Venice: Monti & Compagno, 1736), 3:147–73. Also see Weinberg, *Literary Criticism*, 1:602–3.

16. For Cintio see note 6. For Pigna see Giovanni Battista Nicolucci, called Pigna, *I Romanzi* (Vinegia: Valgrisi, 1554).

17. Discussed in Weinberg, *Literary Criticism*, 2:960–61.

18. For Speroni, see a minor work, "De' Romanzi" in Sperone Speroni, *Opere* (Venice: D. Occhi, 1740), 5:521 ff. For Minturno, see note 2.

19. For an interpretation emphasizing the Neoplatonic aspects of Tasso's thought here, see Phillip Damon, "History and Idea in Renaissance Criticism," in *Literary Criticism and Historical Understanding: Selected Papers from the English Institute* (New York: Columbia University Press, 1967).

20. Torquato Tasso, *Le Lettere*, ed. Guasti (Florence: Le Monnier, 1854), 1:144–48.

21. Tasso develops this argument elaborately in the *Allegoria del poema* written quickly in 1576 after completion of *La Gerusalemme liberata* and published with the second edition in 1581. See Tasso, *Prose diverse*, 1:301–8.

22. Tasso, *Lettere*, 1:102.

23. For such criticism, see Weinberg, *Literary Criticism*, vol. 1, chaps. 7 and 8, pp. 250–348.

24. In the second version of the *Discorsi* (Book V), Tasso cites examples from Dante in his discussion of allegory. For detailed discussion of Tasso's use of the *Commedia* in *La Gerusalemme liberata*, see Dante Della Terza, "Tasso e Dante," *Belfagor*, 25, no. 4 (July 1970):395–418.

25. For detailed discussion of the controversy see Weinberg, vol. 2, chaps. 16 and 17, pp. 819–911. Among the contemporary works, see especially Jacopo Mazzoni, *Discorso in difesa della "Commedia" del divino poeta Dante* (1572), ed. Rossi (Città di Castello: S. Lapi, 1898).

26. Dante Alighieri, *The Divine Comedy*, trans. Charles S. Singleton (Princeton, N.J.: Princeton University Press, 1970). All quotations are from this translation with facing text—substantially the authoritative edition of Giorgio Petrocchi: Dante Alighieri, *La Commedia secondo l'antica vulgata* (Milan: Mondadori, 1966–67).

27. See Michael Murrin, *The Veil of Allegory*, (Chicago: University of Chicago Press, 1969).

28. Isabel G. MacCaffrey, *Spenser's Allegory: The Anatomy of Imagination* (Princeton, N.J.: Princeton University Press, 1976), p. 14.

29. See M. H. Abrams, *The Mirror and the Lamp: Romantic Theory and the Critical Tradition* (London and New York: Oxford University Press, 1953; repr. 1971), pp. 272–85.

30. See Thomas M. Greene, *The Descent from Heaven: A Study in Epic Continuity* (New Haven, Conn.: Yale University Press, 1963), pp. 208–13.

31. William Collins, "An Ode on the Popular Superstitions of the Highlands of Scotland, considered as the Subject of Poetry," stanza 12, in *Poems*, ed. Christopher Stone (London: Milford, 1937), pp. 66–72. I am indebted to Geoffrey Hartman's "False Themes and Gentle Minds," in *Beyond Formalism* (New Haven, Conn.: Yale University Press, 1970), p. 284, for calling my attention to this poem.

32. One crucial symptom of such strain can be seen in the episodes of celestial messengers, analyzed convincingly by Greene in *The Descent from Heaven*. As he demonstrates, there, the very language designed to create vital links between God and man paradoxically expresses the distance separating the two orders of being (pp. 191–93).

33. Quotations are from Giangiorgio Trissino, *L'Italia liberata dai goti* (Parisi: Cavelier, 1729).

34. Tasso, *Lettere*, 1:200–201.

35. Quotations are from Bernardo Tasso, *L'Amadigi* (Venice: Zoppini, 1583).

36. For *Rinaldo* with preface "A'Lettori," see Tasso, *Opere*, ed. Bonfigli, vol. 1 (Bari: Laterza, 1936).

37. See Sozzi, "La Poetica del Tasso," p. 12, and Eugenio Donadoni, *Torquato Tasso*, 4th ed. (Florence: La Nuova Italia, 1952), pp. 57–58.

38. See C. P. Brand, *Torquato Tasso* (Cambridge: at the University Press, 1965), pp. 61–67.

Chapter 2

1. Tasso, *Differenze poetiche*; see chap. 1, note 13.

2. See Morton W. Bloomfield, "Authenticating Realism and the Realism of Chaucer," in *Essays and Explorations* (Cambridge, Mass.: Harvard University Press, 1970), pp. 175–98, for general commentary on this need in narrative art. ". . . the feeling that a tale must be or claim to be true . . . is something absolutely basic to narrative art" (p. 181).

3. See William Nelson, *Fact or Fiction: The Dilemma of the Renaissance Storyteller* (Cambridge, Mass.: Harvard University Press, 1973).

4. Tasso, *Prose diverse*, ed. Guasti.

5. See *Discorsi*, p. 22. In the discussion of the proper size for an epic, Tasso says the criterion should be "la memoria comune degli uomini" and a bit further on, "una mediocre memoria."

Chapter 3

1. Ludovico Ariosto, *Orlando furioso*, ed. Seroni (Milan: Mursia, 1961).

2. "Ottava rima"—an 8-line stanza with rhyme scheme abababcc.

3. Lucretius, *De Rerum Natura*, Loeb Classical Library (Cambridge, Mass.: Harvard University Press, 1953), 1:935–50.

4. A. B. Giamatti, in *The Earthly Paradise and Renaissance Epic* (Princeton, N.J.: Princeton University Press, 1966), notes that the way to Armida's garden is progressively "deeper into the classical past" (p. 193).

5. Tasso, *Le Lettere*, 1:119–20.

6. Giovanni Getto, *Nel mondo della "Gerusalemme"* (Florence: Vallecchi, 1968), p. 82.

7. Francesco De Sanctis, *Storia della letteratura italiana*, ed. Benedetto Croce (Bari: Laterza, 1939), 2:136–75; Benedetto Croce, *La letteratura italiana*, ed. Sansone (Bari: Laterza, 1959), pp. 493–524; Eugenio Donadoni, *Torquato Tasso* (Florence: La Nuora Italia, 1952).

8. See, for example, C. M. Bowra, *From Virgil to Milton* (London: Macmillan, 1963); Graham Hough, *A Preface to "The Faerie Queene"* (New York: Norton, 1962); E. M. W. Tillyard, *The English Epic and its Background* (New York: Oxford University Press, 1966); C. P. Brand, *Torquato Tasso* (Cambridge: at the University Press, 1965).

9. Reuben A. Brower, Introduction to *The Iliad of Homer* translated by Alexander Pope (New York: Macmillan, 1965), p. 20.

10. See the whole section of "Malebolge" (*Inferno*, 18–26), especially cantos 21 and 22.

11. This comparison was noted in an early critical work, the *Comparazione di Omero, Virgilio, e Torquato* of Paolo Beni (1607), whose point was the superiority of Tasso over the classical poets, because his heroes were morally superior. He says that Tasso deliberately modeled Alete and Argante on Ulysses and Achilles to show that the classical characters are not examples of great heroes, but of morally inferior, incomplete characters. ". . . voglio io persuadermi, che il tuo Torquato a bello studio ci dispingesse i due Ambasciatori del Re d'Egitto, Alete, dico, ed Argante, coll'insegne (per così dire) e colori di Ulisse ed Achille, per mostrar, con pace di Omero, che que' colori ed insegne non fossero di saggio e vero Eroe, ma ben d'astuto messaggiero, o superbo campione. . . ." Paolo Beni, *Comparazione di Omero, Virgilio, e Torquato, in* Opere di Tasso, VIII (Venice, 1738), p. 344.

12. Cf. Mezentius in *Aeneid* X, 773–74 (Cambridge, Mass.: Harvard University Press, Loeb Classical Library, 1967), "dextra mihi deus et telum, quod missile libro,/nunc adsint!"

13. The classical association is reinforced by the echo of the fury, Allecto's hurling of her torch to kindle the rage of Turnus in *Aeneid* VII, 445–62.

14. Donadoni, *Torquato Tasso*, chap. 12.

15. I am indebted in this and the following paragraph to the excellent chapter by Giovanni Getto, "La Tragedia di Solimano," in *Nel mondo della "Gerusalemme."*

16. See ibid.

Chapter 4

1. In Canto IV, for instance, when Armida seduces the warriors to follow her away from the Christian camp, there is constant repetition of *errare* and *smarrito* (lost). In this same

verbal context, the warriors use the traditional chivalric code as justification for their desertion of the cause. Smarrito is rich in moral connotation from its use in the *Divina commedia*.

Chapter 5

1. E.g., a letter of 15 April 1575 to Scipione Gonzaga: ". . . io so molto bene d'essermi dilatato assai più di Virgilio e d'Omero, procurando di dilettare; ma . . . stimo però che questa latitudine, per così dirla, sia ristretta dentro a i termini d'unità d'azione almeno, se non d'uomo: benchè i molti cavalieri sono considerati nel mio poema come membra d'un corpo, del quale è capo Goffredo, Rinaldo destra; sì che in un certo modo si può dire anco unità d'agente, non che d'azione" (Tasso, *Lettere*, 1:65).

2. See Tasso, *Lettere*, vol. 1, no. 32 (7 June 1575) to Luca Scalabrino, pp. 81–89; no. 37 (27 June 1575) to Scipione Gonzaga, pp. 95–96; no. 38 (5 July 1575) to Scipione Gonzaga, pp. 96–98.

3. Armida, armed as a Diana (XX, 68), creates echoes of the beloved huntress, Silvia, in Tasso's *Aminta*, his poem of sensual idyll and pleasure in the varieties of love poetry.

4. Giovanni Getto notes (*Nel mondo della "Gerusalemme,"* p. 214): "La bella incantatrice non strappa solo il cavaliere al campo cristiano, segnando un vuoto incolmabile nella vicenda militare, ma costituisce pure una tentazione per il poeta, determinando una specie di rottura di equilibrio nel piano compositivo della *Gerusalemme*. I canti XIV, XV, XVI rappresentano la più sontuosa vacanza per la fantasia del Tasso lungo l'itinerario del poema della crociata."

5. I am indebted in this paragraph to the chapter on Tasso in Robert M. Durling, *The Figure of the Poet in Renaissance Epic* (Cambridge, Mass.: Harvard University Press, 1965).

6. See for instance no. 25 of 15 April 1575 to Scipione Gonzaga, where he is worried about how to turn from the subject of Armida to the fight between Rinaldo and Gernando (Tasso, *Lettere*, 1:63–68).

7. Durling, *Figure of the Poet*, p. 205.

8. See C. M. Bowra, *From Virgil to Milton* (London: Macmillan, 1963), p. 184: ". . . his treatment of Armida is implicitly a criticism of the liberty which the Renaissance had allowed and the Counter-Reformation denied. . . . Tasso himself sometimes looked back to the Renaissance with regretful longing. . . . It was for him in some ways a Golden Age. . . . Tasso knew this appeal but renounced it, and made the desire for such freedom a temptation. . . ."

9. Cf. "otium" in Virgil, *Eclogues* 1.6ff. (Cambridge, Mass.: Harvard University Press, 1935).

10. N.b. the association and thus pointed contrast with Dido in *Aeneid* IV, 23, "adgnosco veteris vestigia flammae."

11. "Non fu mai greca, o barbara, o latina/ Progenie, in questo o nel buon tempo antico,/ Ricca di tanti eroi quanti destina/ A te chiari neopti il Cielo amico;/ Ch'agguaglieran qual più chiaro si noma/ Di Sparta, di Cartagine e di Roma" (XVII, 89).

12. Bowra, *From Virgil to Milton*, p. 153.

13. See Fredi Chiappelli, *Studi sul linguaggio del Tasso epico* (Florence: Le Monnier, 1957), pp. 5–6, 15.

Chapter 6

1. See F. T. Prince, *The Italian Element in Milton's Verse* (Oxford: Clarendon Press, 1954); Mario Praz, *The Flaming Heart* (Garden City, N.Y.: Doubleday Anchor Books, 1958); Douglas Bush, *John Milton* (New York: Macmillan, 1964); E. M. W. Tillyard, *The English Epic and Its Background*; C. M. Bowra, *From Virgil to Milton*; (London: Macmillan, 1963) J. B. Broadbent, *Some Graver Subject* (London: Chatto & Windus, 1970);

John M. Steadman, *Milton and the Renaissance Hero* (Oxford: Clarendon Press, 1967);
C. P. Brand, *Torquato Tasso* (Cambridge: at the University Press, 1965). John M. Steadman in *Epic and Tragic Structure in "Paradise Lost"* (Chicago: University of Chicago Press,
1976) argues for the relevance of sixteenth-century Italian criticism for an understanding of
Milton's epic.

2. Many critics have noted this—among them Douglas Bush; C. M. Bowra; Gilbert
Highet in *The Classical Tradition* (New York: Oxford University Press, 1957); Isabel G.
MacCaffrey in *"Paradise Lost" as "Myth"* (Cambridge, Mass.: Harvard University Press,
1959); Anne D. Ferry in *Milton's Epic Voice* (Cambridge, Mass.: Harvard University Press,
1963); Burton O. Kurth in *Milton and Christian Heroism* (Hamden, Conn.: Archon
Books, 1966); J. B. Broadbent; Northrop Frye in *The Return of Eden* (Toronto: University
of Toronto Press, 1965); and John M. Steadman.

3. See Stanley E. Fish, *Surprised by Sin* (London: Macmillan, 1967), pp. 162–80 for
discussion of Milton's condemnation of the idea that war is heroic. Fish is right (p. 168) to
see Milton toppling the "scaffolding of Tasso's *Jerusalem Delivered*" in the simile when he
includes the wars of "baptized or infidel" in his devaluation of military action. But Milton
here rejects Tasso's solution to the problem of Christian heroism (to transform the physical
battle into a *holy* war) only by extension. The comparison explicitly refers, not to Tasso, but
to Ariosto, Boiardo, and Pulci. Since Milton here dismisses literary celebrations of warfare
with a long roll call of suggestive names, his decision *not* to include a name specifically
related to *La Gerusalemme liberata* perhaps indicates greater unease at directly associating
Tasso's poem with the literature of false heroism.

4. "Milton's 'heroic' archfiend turns out to be an ingenious literary device for reassessing
the heroic tradition. The paradox of a 'godlike' devil enables him to arraign epic and history
alike for mistaking brutishness for heroic virtue, and thus celebrating the counterfeit idol of
heroism." Steadman, *Milton and the Renaissance Hero*, p. 174.

5. Ibid., p. xx.

6. Steadman (in *Milton and the Renaissance Hero*) mentions the contrast between Aeneas
and Turnus as an example of a limited critique of this kind and also remarks that Tasso "had
obliquely censured the Homeric heroes by transferring their traits to inferiors and infidels"
(p. 17), though he seems to see Tasso doing this only in the limited context of the episode in
Canto II of the embassy of Argante and Alete to the Christian camp.

7. See ibid., p. 18.

8. "The continuous parallel between the fall of the angels and the fall of man is, of course,
one of the major structural and moral principles of the poem . . ." MacCaffrey, *"Paradise
Lost" as "Myth,"* p. 181.

9. Steadman's phrase, *Milton and the Renaissance Hero*, p. 193.

10. For discussion of the narrative persona in *Paradise Lost*, see Ferry, *Milton's Epic
Voice*.

11. MacCaffrey, *"Paradise Lost" as "Myth,"* p. 56.

12. See Joseph E. Duncan, *Milton's Earthly Paradise* (Minneapolis: University of Minnesota Press, 1972), pp. 9 ff. Also see Basil Willey, *The Seventeenth Century Background*
(1934); reprinted, Garden City, N.Y.: Doubleday Anchor Books), chap. 4.

13. See Ferry, *Milton's Epic Voice*, p. 92–93.

14. See MacCaffrey, *"Paradise Lost" as "Myth,"* pp. 56–68.

15. Ibid., pp. 188–90.

16. Previous students of Milton's relationship to Tasso's poetry in *Paradise Lost* have
considered the *Gerusalemme liberata* to have been "of limited value" to him, even in the
area of style where the only substantial affinity has been seen. See F. T. Prince, *The Italian
Element in Milton's Verse*, p. 50; Mario Praz, *The Flaming Heart*; C. P. Brand, *Torquato
Tasso*. Praz argues, p. 326, that *Paradise Lost* comes much closer to Tasso's theoretical
stylistic ideal of "magnificence" and "music" than anything in Tasso's poetry. He states that
Tasso's importance for Milton lies almost wholly in the precepts of the *Discorsi*. Prince, in
"Milton e Tasso," *Rivista di letterature moderne e comparate* 13 (1960):53–60, repeats his
assertion of the importance of *Le sette giornate del mondo creato* rather than *La
Gerusalemme liberata* for the development of Milton's blank verse.

17. Patrick Cullen in *Infernal Triad: The Flesh, the World, and the Devil in Spenser and Milton* (Princeton, N.J.: Princeton University Press, 1974) has argued for close thematic and structural connections between *The Faerie Queene* and *Paradise Lost*.

18. "Milton was the Poetical Son of Spencer. . . . Milton has acknowledged to me, that Spencer was his Original. . . ." John Dryden in "Preface" to *Fables Ancient and Modern*, in *The Poems and Fables of John Dryden*, ed. James Kinsley (London: Oxford University Press, 1962) p. 521.

19. See Christopher Ricks, *Milton's Grand Style* (Oxford: The Clarendon Press, 1963), pp. 63ff.

20. It is interesting to note that Spenser had also evoked etymological associations to invest his language with moral, emotional, and spiritual connotations. See Martha Craig, "The Secret Wit of Spenser's Language," in Paul J. Alpers, ed., *Elizabethan Poetry: Modern Essays in Criticism* (New York: Oxford University Press, 1967) reprinted in Paul J. Alpers, ed., *Edmund Spenser* (Baltimore, Md.: Penguin Books, 1969).

21. See Isabel G. MacCaffrey, *Spenser's Allegory* (Princeton, N.J.: Princeton University Press, 1976). pp. 60–61.

22. Ibid., pp. 13–32.

23. All quotations of *The Faerie Queene* are from *The Poetical Works of Edmund Spenser*, ed. J. C. Smith and E. de Selincourt (London: Oxford University Press, 1912; repr. 1961).

24. A. B. Giamatti in *The Earthly Paradise and the Renaissance Epic* (Princeton, N.J.: Princeton University Press, 1966) suggests that "in a garden we are at the heart of a poem and the problems it poses . . ." (p. 6).

25. See ibid., pp. 126ff.

26. See notes to Book IV of *Paradise Lost* in the Fowler-Cary edition for many examples. See also the brief discussion in John R. Knott, Jr., *Milton's Pastoral Vision* (Chicago: The University of Chicago Press, 1971), p. 34, p. 48, and detailed discussion in Giamatti, *Earthly Paradise*, chap. 6.

27. C. S. Lewis, *The Allegory of Love* (London: Oxford University Press, 1936; repr. 1958), p. 304.

28. For an extended comparative discussion of these two episodes, see Robert M. Durling, "The Bower of Bliss and Armida's Palace," in *Comparative Literature* 6 (1954): 335–47.

29. Milton, *Areopagitica*, in *Complete Prose Works of John Milton*, 2:516.

30. Alastair Fowler, "Emblems of Temperance in *The Faerie Queene*, Book II," *Review of English Studies*, n.s. 2 (1960):143–49.

31. See Arlene N. Okerlund, "Spenser's Wanton Maidens: Reader Psychology and the Bower of Bliss," *PMLA* 88, no. 1 (January 1973):62–69, for discussion of the sensual impact on readers.

32. Durling, for other interpretive purposes, emphasizes the difference between Tasso's "magic" made to look like nature in the garden and Spenser's "artifice" in the Bower.

33. See Duncan, *Milton's Earthly Paradise*, especially chaps. 5 and 6.

34. In Tasso (XVI, 10–11) the fruits and colors are specified, creating a more particular and delimited image.

35. This is the only use of *luxuriant* in Milton's poetry. See William Ingram and Kathleen Swain, eds., *A Concordance to Milton's English Poetry* (Oxford: Clarendon Press, 1972). Its cognates, *luxury* and *luxurious*, appear several times in *Paradise Lost*, always as moral pejoratives except at the equivocal moment in Book IX, 209. The use of *luxuriant* here provides minute but striking confirmation of Milton's intimate familiarity with *La Gerusalemme liberata* in Italian, as Fairfax leaves out this adjective completely in his translation of Tasso's stanza. See *Jerusalem Delivered*, trans. Edward Fairfax (New York: Capricorn Books, 1963). But see also A. B. Giamatti, "Milton and Fairfax's Tasso" in *Revue de littérature comparée* 40, no. 4 (1966):613–15, for several examples of possible borrowings from Fairfax in *Paradise Lost*.

36. Tasso, *Rime d'amore*, Libro II, no. cxliii, in *Opere di Torquato Tasso*, ed. Petrocchi (Milan: Mursia, 1961); Claudio Monteverdi, *Il secondo libro di madrigali* (1590) in *Tutte le opere di Claudio Monteverdi*, ed. Francesco Malipiero (Asolo, 1926–42), vol. 2.

37. See Harry Levin, *The Myth of the Golden Age in the Renaissance* (New York: Oxford University Press, 1972), p. 138.

38. Tasso, *Aminta*, in *Opere di Torquato Tasso*, ed. Petrocchi.

39. This is argued by Ricks, *Milton's Grand Style*, pp. 109–13, and by Arnold Stein, *Answerable Style* (Seattle: University of Washington Press, 1967), pp. 66–67.

40. This is suggested by the word order of the poem's title.

41. See Ricks, *Milton's Grand Style*, pp. 112ff. and 145ff. He uses the example of the stream "wandering" (IV, 234) "with mazy error under pendant shades" (IV, 239), following Stein, *Answerable Style*, pp. 66ff. But see also Giamatti in *The Earthly Paradise and Renaissance Epic*, pp. 302ff, who argues that the postlapsarian perspective is exploited by the poet to suggest latent possibilities in perfect nature. Fish in *Surprised by Sin*, pp. 101–3, argues that Milton deliberately evokes the fallen meanings of *wanton, error*, etc. as part of a strategy to arouse the readers's awareness of his own sin.

42. See further the uses of *naked* and *bare* in IX, 1056–75.

43. Geoffrey Hartman's term in *Beyond Formalism*, p. 284.

44. See Jackson I. Cope, *The Metaphoric Structure of Paradise Lost* (Baltimore, Md.: Johns Hopkins Press, 1962), pp. 124–26, for discussion of the governing paradox that physical sight becomes spiritual blindness, while physical blindness is converted by God to spiritual "insight."

45. See Anne Ferry, *Milton's Epic Voice*, chap. 1.

46. Irene Samuel, in *Dante and Milton* (Ithaca, N.Y.: Cornell University Press, 1966), does not discuss this issue, though she compares the two poets' exordia in some detail.

47. I would argue that this is also true of what appears to be an even more Dantesque description of the narrator in the invocation to Book VII ("Up led by thee / Into the heaven of heavens I have presumed, / An earthly guest . . ." VII, 12–14), because of the insistently literary language with which he defines his flight.

48. Geoffrey Hartman, *Beyond Formalism*, p. 143. "Sight and light are mediated by the word, even as Milton's poem is basically words about the Word: an inspired commentary on Scripture."

49. Reading Scripture for Milton, of course, meant Scripture and commentaries. See Arnold Williams, *The Common Expositor: An Account of the Commentaries on Genesis, 1527–1633* (Chapel Hill: University of North Carolina Press, 1948). Moreover, he is drawing on the long hexameral tradition in his interpretation of Genesis. See J. M. Evans, *"Paradise Lost" and the Genesis Tradition* "Oxford: Clarendon Press, 1968); Sister M. I. Corcoran, *Milton's Paradise with Reference to the Hexaemeral Background* (Washington, D.C.: Catholic University of America Press, 1945); Duncan, *Milton's Earthly Paradise*. My point is that he has *chosen* to use the most inclusive tradition, in which a great deal must be brought together by the teller.

50. William G. Madsen in *From Shadowy Types to Truth* (New Haven, Conn.: Yale University Press, 1968), pp. 145–80, sets *Paradise Lost* in the context of Puritan preference for the ear over the eye, for hearing the word over sight. He shows the particular resonance for seventeenth-century Protestants, and Milton in particular, of St. Paul's "Faith is by hearing" (Romans 10:17) and "we walk by faith, and not by sight" (2 Corinthians 5:7). See also Barbara K. Lewalski, "Structure and the Symbolism of Vision in Michael's Prophecy, *Paradise Lost*, Books XI–XII," *Philological Quarterly* 42 (1963):25–35.

51. Barbara K. Lewalski in *Milton's Brief Epic* (Providence, R.I.: Brown University Press; London: Methuen, 1966), pp. 3–129, has shown that *Paradise Regained* belongs to a different "epic" tradition with other predecessors, notably the Book of Job. It therefore does not invite the same generic associations as *Paradise Lost*.

Appendix

La Gerusalemme liberata, XV, 55–62

Canto XV

55   I cavalier per l'alta aspra salita
Sentìansi alquanto affaticati e lassi;
Onde ne gìan per quella via fiorita
Lenti or movendo ed or fermando i passi:
Quando ecco un fonte, che a bagnar gl'invita
L'asciutte labbia, alto cader da' sassi
E da una larga vena, e con ben mille
Zampilletti spruzzar l'erbe di stille.

      The knights, because of the steep, difficult climb
Feel somewhat weary and weak;
So they go along that flowery path
Slowly, now moving now arresting their steps:
When suddenly a fountain appears, that invites them to bathe
Their dry lips, falling from rocks high above
In a broad stream, sprinkling the grass
With a thousand jets of spray.

56   Ma tutta insieme poi tra verdi sponde
In profondo canal l'acqua s'aduna;
E sotto l'ombra di perpetue fronde
Mormorando sen va gelida e bruna,
Ma trasparente sì, che non asconde
De l'imo letto suo vaghezza alcuna:
E sovra le sue rive alta s'estolle
L'erbetta, e vi fa seggio fresco e molle.

      But then all together through the green banks
The water unites into a deep channel

And beneath the shade of everlasting branches
Passes murmuring, cold and dark;
But so transparent that nothing is hidden
Of all the loveliness of its bed,
And above its banks grow high
Grasses that make a fresh, soft seat.

57   —Ecco il fonte del riso, ed ecco il rio
Che mortali perigli in sé contiene;
Or qui tener a fren nostro desio,
Ed esser cauti molto a noi conviene;
Chiudiam l'orecchie al dolce canto e rio
Di queste del piacer false Sirene;
Così n'andrem sin dove il fiume vago
Si spande in maggior letto, e forma un lago.—

    "Here is the fountain of laughter, and here is the stream [rio]
That holds mortal dangers (dangers to mortals);
Now here it is most necessary for us to rein in
Our desire and be prudent;
Let us close our ears to the sweet, evil [rio] song
Of these false Sirens of pleasure;
So let us go where the lovely river
spreads out into a larger bed and forms a lake."

58   Quivi di cibi prezïosa e cara
Apprestata è una mensa in su le rive:
E scherzando sen van per l'acqua chiara
Due donzellette garrule e lascive,
Ch'or si spruzzano il vólto, or fanno a gara
Chi prima a un segno destinato arrive:
Si tuffano talora, e 'l capo e 'l dorso
Scopron al fin dopo il celato corso.

    Here a lavish, exquisite table full of
Foods is readied on the bank:
And in the clear water play
Two laughing, wanton maidens,
Now splashing each other's faces, now contesting
Who can reach a goal first:
Sometimes they dive, and finally reveal head
And back after the hidden swim.

59   Mosser le natatrici ignude e belle
De' duo guerrieri alquanto i duri petti,
Sì che fermârsi a riguardarle; ed elle
Seguìan pur i lor giuochi e i lor diletti.

Una in tanto drizzossi, e le mammelle
E tutto ciò che più la vista alletti
Mostrò, dal seno in suso, aperto al cielo,
E 'l lago a l'altre membra era un bel velo.

> The beautiful, naked swimmers moved
> Somewhat the rigid hearts [chests] of the two warriors,
> So that they stopped to look at them; and they
> Continued their games and pleasures.
> One stood upright, and showed her breasts
> And everything that most delights the eye,
> From the chest downward, open to the sky,
> And the lake was a lovely veil for the other parts.

60   Qual matutina stella da l'onde
Rugiadosa e stillante; o come fuore
Spuntò, nascendo già da le feconde
Spume de l'oceàn, la dea d'amore;
Tal apparve costei; tal le sue bionde
Chiome stillavan cristallino umore.
Poi girò gli occhi, e pur allor s'infinse
Que' duo vedere, e in sé tutta si strinse:

> Like the morning star [rising] dewy and sparkling
> From the waves; or as when, newborn
> From the fruitful foam of ocean,
> The goddess of love rose up;
> So she appeared; just so her blond
> Hair was sparkling with crystalline liquid.
> Then she turned her eyes, and at that moment pretended
> To see the two of them, and drew back into herself:

61   E 'l crin, ch'in cima al capo avea raccolto
In un sol nodo, immantinente sciolse,
Che lunghissimo in giù cadendo e folto,
D'un aureo manto i molli avori involse.
Oh che vago spettacolo è lor tolto!
Ma non men vago fu chi loro il tolse
Così da l'acque e da' capelli ascosa
A lor si volse lieta e vergognosa.

> And her hair, which had been gathered on top of her head
> In a single knot, she immediately let loose
> So that, falling in the longest, thick folds
> It covered the soft ivories with a golden mantle.
> Oh what a beautiful spectacle was taken from them!
> But not less beautiful was she who took it from them.

Thus hidden by water and hair
She turned to them, gay and bashful.

62   Rideva insieme, e insieme ella arrossìa;
        Ed era nel rossor più bello il riso,
        E nel riso il rossor che le coprìa
        In sino al mento il delicato viso.
        Mosse la voce poi sì dolce e pia,
        Che fôra ciascun altro indi conquiso:
        —Oh fortunati peregrin, cui lice
        Giungere in questa sede alma e felice!

She laughed and blushed together;
And by the blushing color her laughter became more beautiful,
As by the laughter the blush that covered
Her exquisite face to the chin.
Then she raised her sweet, gentle voice,
That would have conquered any other at that moment:
"Oh fortunate wayfarers, permitted
To arrive at this bountiful, happy place of rest!

The Faerie Queene, II, xii, 60–68

Book II, Canto xii

60   And in the midst of all, a fountaine stood,
            Of richest substaunce, that on earth might bee,
            So pure and shiny, that the siluer flood
            Through euery channell running one might see;
            Most goodly it with curious imageree
            Was ouer-wrought, and shapes of naked boyes,
            Of which some seemd with liuely iollitee,
            To fly about, playing their wanton toyes,
        Whilest others did them selues embay in liquid ioyes.

61   And ouer all, of purest gold was spred,
            A trayle of yuie in his natiue hew:
            For the rich metall was so coloured,
            That wight, who did not well auis'd it vew,
            Would surely deeme it to be yuie trew:
            Low his lasciuious armes adown did creepe,
            That themselues dipping in the siluer dew,
            Their fleecy flowres they tenderly did steepe,
        Which drops of Christall seemd for wantones to weepe.

62   Infinit streames continually did well
        Out of this fountaine, sweet and faire to see,
        The which into an ample lauer fell,
        And shortly grew to so great quantitie,
        That like a little lake it seemd to bee;
        Whose depth exceeded not three cubits hight,
        That through the waues one might the bottom see,
        All pau'd beneath with Iaspar shining bright,
     That seemd the fountaine in that sea did sayle vpright.

63   And all the margent round about was set,
        With shady Laurell trees, thence to defend
        The sunny beames, which on the billowes bet,
        And those which therein bathed, mote offend.
        As Guyon hapned by the same to wend,
        Two naked Damzelles he therein espyde,
        Which therin bathing, seemed to contend,
        And wrestle wantonly, ne car'd to hyde
     Their dainty parts from vew of any, which them eyde.

64   Sometimes the one would lift the other quight
        Aboue the waters, and then downe againe
        Her plong, as ouer maistered by might,
        Where both awhile would couered remaine,
        And each the other from to rise restraine;
        The whiles their snowy limbes, as through a vele,
        So through the Christall waues appeared plaine:
        Then suddeinly both would themselues vnhele,
     And th'amarous sweet spoiles to greedy eyes reuele.

65   As that faire Starre, the messenger of morne,
        His deawy face out of the sea doth reare:
        Or as the Cyprian goddesse, newly borne
        Of th'Oceans fruitfull froth, did first appear:
        Such seemed they, and so their yellow heare
        Christalline humour dropped downe apace.
        Whomsuch when Guyon saw, he drew him neare,
        And somewhat gan relent his earnest pace,
     His stubborne brest gan secret pleasaunce to embrace.

66   The wanton Maidens him espying, stood
        Gazing a while at his vnwonted guise;
        Then th'one her selfe low ducked in the flood,
        Abasht, that her a straunger did a vise;

But th'other rather higher did arise,
And her two lilly paps aloft displayd,
And all, that might his melting hart entise
To her delights, she vnto him bewrayd:
The rest hid vnderneath, him more desirous made.

67　With that, the other likewise vp arose,
And her faire lockes, which formerly were bownd
Vp in one knot, she low adowne did lose:
Which flowing long and thick, her cloth'd arownd,
And th'yuorie in golden mantle gownd:
So that faire spectacle from him was reft,
Yet that, which reft it, no lesse faire was fownd:
So hid in lockes and waues from lookers theft,
Nought but her louely face she for his looking left.

68　Withall she laughed, and she blusht withall,
That blushing to her laughter gaue more grace,
And laughter to her blushing, as did fall:
Now when they spide the knight to slacke his pace,
Them to behold, and in his sparkling face
The secret signes of kindled lust appeare,
Their wanton meriments they did encreace,
And to him beckned, to approch more neare,
And shewd him many sights, that courage cold could reare.

Bibliography

Primary Sources

Ariosto, Ludovico. *Orlando furioso.* Edited by Adriano Seroni. Milano: Mursia, 1961.

Beni, Paolo. *Comparazione di Omero, Virgilio, e Torquato* (1607). In Torquato Tasso, *Opere di Tasso,* vol. 8. Venezia, 1738.

Cintio, Giraldi G. G. (Cinthio) *On Romances.* Translated by Henry L. Snuggs. Lexington: University of Kentucky Press, 1968.

———. (Cinzio). *Scritti critici.* Edited by C. G. Crocetti. Milano: Marzorati, 1973.

Collins, William. "An Ode on the Popular Superstitions of the Highlands of Scotland, considered as the Subject of Poetry." In *Poems,* edited by Christopher Stone. London: Milford, 1937.

Dante. *The Divine Comedy.* Translated by Charles S. Singleton. Princeton, N.J.: Princeton University Press, 1970.

Dryden, John. "Preface" to *Fables Ancient and Modern.* In *The Poems and Fables of John Dryden,* edited by James Kinsley. London: Oxford University Press, 1962.

Horace. *Ars Poetica.* Translated by H. R. Fairclough. Loeb Classical Library. Cambridge, Mass.: Harvard University Press, 1929.

Lucretius. *De Rerum Natura.* Translated by W. H. D. Rouse. Loeb Classical Library. Cambridge, Mass.: Harvard University Press, 1953.

Mazzoni, Jacopo. *Discorso in difesa della "Commedia" del divino poeta Dante* (1572). Edited by Mario Rossi. Città di Castello: S. Lapi, 1898.

Milton, John. *The Poems of Milton.* Edited by John Carey and Alastair Fowler. London: Longmans, 1968.

———. *Complete Prose Works of John Milton.* Edited by Douglas Bush et al. New Haven, Conn.: Yale University Press, 1953.

171

Minturno, Antonio. *L'arte poetica.* Venice: Valvassori, 1563.

Monteverdi, Claudio. *Il secondo libro di madrigali* (1590). In *Tutte le opere di Claudio Monteverdi,* edited by Francesco Malipiero, vol. 2. Asolo, 1926–42.

Nicolucci (Pigna), Giovanni Battista. *I Romanzi.* Vinegia: Valgrisi, 1554.

Patrizi, Francesco. *Parere di Francesco Patrizi in difesa di Lodovico Ariosto.* In Torquato Tasso, *Opere,* vol. 3. Venice: Monti e Compagno, 1736.

Plato. *Laws.* Translated by R. G. Bury. Loeb Classical Library. Cambridge, Mass.: Harvard University Press, 1952.

Spenser, Edmund. *The Poetical Works of Edmund Spenser.* Edited by J. C. Smith and E. de Selincourt. London: Oxford University Press, 1912; repr. 1961.

Speroni, Sperone. *De' Romanzi.* In Sperone Speroni, *Opere,* vol. 5 Venice: D. Occhi, 1740.

Tasso, Bernardo. *L'Amadigi.* Venice: Zoppini, 1583.

———. *Ragionamento della poesia.* In *Lettere di M. Bernardo Tasso,* vol. 2, Padua: Comino, 1733.

Tasso, Torquato. *La Gerusalemme liberata.* Edited by L. Magugliani. Milan: Rizzoli, 1950.

———. *Jerusalem Delivered.* Translated by Edward Fairfax. 1600. Reprint. New York: Capricorn Books, 1963.

———. *Discorsi dell'arte poetica e del poema eroico.* Edited by Luigi Poma. Bari: Laterza, 1964.

———. *Discourses on the Heroic Poem.* Translated by I. Samuel and M. Cavalchini. Oxford: Clarendon Press, 1973.

———. *Le Lettere.* Edited by C. Guasti. Florence: Le Monnier, 1854.

———. *Lezione sopra il sonetto: Questa vita mortal ec. di Monsignor della Casa.* In *Opere,* vol. 6. Venice: Monti e Compagno, 1736.

———. *Rinaldo.* In *Opere,* edited by Luigi Bonfigli, vol. 1. Bari: Laterza, 1936.

———. "Allegoria del poema". In *Prose diverse,* edited by C. Guasti, vol. 1. Florence, 1875.

———. *Discorso di Torquato Tasso sopra il parere fatto dal signor Francesco Patricio in difesa di Lodovico Ariosto.* in *Opere,* vol. 3. Venice: Monti e Compagno, 1736.

———. *Del giudizio sovra la Gerusalemme di Torquato Tasso da lui medesimo riformata.* In *Prose diverse,* vol. 1 edited by C. Guasti. Florence, 1875.

———. *Rime d'amore.* In *Opere di Torquato Tasso,* edited by Giorgio Petrocchi. Milan: Mursia, 1961.

———. *Aminta*. In *Opere di Torquato Tasso*, edited by Giorgio Petrocchi. Milan: Mursia, 1961.

Trissino, Giangiorgio. *L'Italia liberata dai goti*. Parigi: Cavelier, 1729.

———. *Poetica*. In *Tutte le opere*, vol. 2. Verona: Vallarsi, 1729.

Vida, Marco Girolamo. *Ars Poetica*. Translated by Pitt. In *The Art of Poetry: The Poetical Treatises of Horace, Vida and Boileau*, edited by A. S. Cook. Boston: Ginn, 1892.

Virgil. *Aeneid*. Translated by H. R. Fairclough. Loeb Classical Library. Cambridge, Mass.: Harvard University Press, 1967.

———. *Eclogues*. Translated by H. R. Fairclough. Loeb Classical Library. Cambridge, Mass.: Harvard University Press, 1935.

Secondary Sources

Abrams, M. H. *The Mirror and the Lamp: Romantic Theory and the Critical Tradition*. London and New York: Oxford University Press, 1953; repr. 1971.

Bloomfield, Morton W. "Authenticating Realism and the Realism of Chaucer." In *Essays and Explorations*. Cambridge, Mass.: Harvard University Press, 1970.

Bowra, C. M. *From Virgil to Milton*. London: Macmillan, 1963.

Brand, C. P. *Torquato Tasso*. Cambridge: At the University Press, 1965.

Brink, C. O. *Horace on Poetry*. Cambridge: At the University Press, 1971.

Broadbent, J. B. *Some Graver Subject*. London: Chatto and Windus, 1970.

Brower, Reuben A. *Hero and Saint: Shakespeare and the Graeco-Roman Heroic Tradition*. New York: Oxford University Press, 1971.

———. "Introduction" in *The Iliad of Homer translated by Alexander Pope*. New York: Macmillan, 1965.

Bush, Douglas. *John Milton*. New York: Macmillan, 1964.

Chiappelli, Fredi. *Studi sul linguaggio del Tasso epico*. Florence: Le Monnier, 1957.

Commager, Steele. *The Odes of Horace*. New Haven, Conn.: Yale University Press, 1962; repr. ed., Bloomington: Indiana University Press, 1967.

Cope, Jackson I. *The Metaphoric Structure of Paradise Lost*. Baltimore, Md.: Johns Hopkins Press, 1962.

Corcoran, Sister M. I. *Milton's Paradise with Reference to the Hexaemeral Background*. Washington, D.C.: Catholic University of America Press, 1945.

Craig, Martha. "The Secret Wit of Spenser's Language." In *Elizabethan Poetry: Modern Essays in Criticism*. New York: Oxford University Press, 1967.

Croce, Benedetto. *La letteratura italiana*. Edited by M. Sansone. Bari: Laterza, 1959.

Cullen, Patrick. *Infernal Triad: The Flesh, the World, and the Devil in Spenser and Milton*. Princeton, N.J.: Princeton University Press, 1974.

Damon, Phillip. "History and Idea in Renaissance Criticism." In *Literary Criticism and Historical Understanding*, edited by Phillip Damon. New York: Columbia University Press, 1967.

Della Terza, Dante. "Tasso e Dante." *Belfagor* 25, no. 4 (July 1970): 395–418.

DeSanctis, Francesco. *Storia della letteratura italiana*. Edited by Benedetto Croce. Bari: Laterza, 1939.

Donadoni, Eugenio. *Torquato Tasso*. Florence: La Nuova Italia, 1952.

Duncan, Joseph E. *Milton's Earthly Paradise*. Minneapolis: University of Minnesota Press, 1972.

Durling, Robert M. *The Figure of the Poet in Renaissance Epic*. Cambridge, Mass.: Harvard University Press, 1965.

———. "The Bower of Bliss and Armida's Palace." *Comparative Literature* 6 (1954): 335–47.

Evans, J. M. *"Paradise Lost" and the Genesis Tradition*. Oxford: Clarendon Press, 1968.

Ferry, Anne D. *Milton's Epic Voice*. Cambridge, Mass.: Harvard University Press, 1963.

Fish, Stanley E. *Surprised by Sin*. London: Macmillan, 1967.

Fowler, Alastair. "Emblems of Temperance in *The Faerie Queene*, Book II." *Review of English Studies*, n.s. 2 (1960): 143–49.

Frye, Northrop. *The Return of Eden*. Toronto: University of Toronto Press, 1965.

Getto, Giovanni. *Nel mondo della "Gerusalemme."* Florence: Vallecchi, 1968.

Giamatti, A. B. *The Earthly Paradise and Renaissance Epic*. Princeton, N.J.: Princeton University Press, 1966.

———. "Milton and Fairfax's Tasso." *Revue de littérature comparée* 40, no. 4 (1966): 613–15.

Gilbert, Allan. *Literary Criticism: Plato to Dryden*. New York: American Book Co., 1940.

Greene, Thomas M. *The Descent from Heaven: A Study in Epic Continuity*. New Haven, Conn.: Yale University Press, 1963.

Hartman, Geoffrey. *Beyond Formalism.* New Haven, Conn.: Yale University Press, 1970.

Hathaway, Baxter. *The Age of Criticism: The Late Renaissance in Italy.* Ithaca, N.Y.: Cornell University Press, 1962.

———. *Marvels and Commonplaces: Renaissance Literary Criticism.* New York: Random House, 1968.

Herrick, Marvin T. *The Fusion of Horatian and Aristotelian Literary Criticism, 1531–1555.* Urbana, Ill.: University of Illinois Press, 1946.

Highet, Gilbert. *The Classical Tradition.* New York: Oxford University Press, 1957.

Hough, Graham. *A Preface to "The Faerie Queene."* New York: Norton, 1962.

Ingram, William and Swain, Kathleen, eds. *A Concordance to Milton's English Poetry.* Oxford: Clarendon Press, 1972.

Knott, John R., Jr. *Milton's Pastoral Vision.* Chicago: University of Chicago Press, 1971.

Kurth, Burton O. *Milton and Christian Heroism.* Hamden, Conn.: Archon Books, 1966.

Levin, Harry. *The Myth of the Golden Age in the Renaissance.* New York: Oxford University Press, 1972.

Lewalski, Barbara K. *Milton's Brief Epic.* Providence, R.I.: Brown University Press, London: Methuen, 1966.

———. "Structure and the Symbolism of Vision in Michael's Prophecy, *Paradise Lost,* Books XI–XII." *Philological Quarterly* 42 (1963): 25–35.

Lewis, C. S. *The Allegory of Love.* London: Oxford University Press, 1936; repr. 1958.

MacCaffrey, Isabel G. *"Paradise Lost" as "Myth."* Cambridge, Mass.: Harvard University Press, 1959.

———. *Spenser's Allegory: The Anatomy of Imagination.* Princeton, N.J.: Princeton University Press, 1976.

Madsen, William G. *From Shadowy Types to Truth.* New Haven, Conn.: Yale University Press, 1968.

Murrin, Michael. *The Veil of Allegory.* Chicago: University of Chicago Press, 1969.

Nelson, William. *Fact or Fiction: The Dilemma of the Renaissance Storyteller.* Cambridge, Mass.: Harvard University Press, 1973.

Okerlund, Arlene N. "Spenser's Wanton Maidens: Reader Psychology and the Bower of Bliss." *PMLA* 88, no. 1 (January 1973): 62–69.

Praz, Mario. *The Flaming Heart.* Garden City, N.Y.: Doubleday, 1958.

Prince, F. T. *The Italian Element in Milton's Verse.* Oxford: Clarendon Press, 1954.

———. "Milton e Tasso." *Rivista di letterature moderne e comparate* 13 (1960): 53–60.

Ricks, Christopher. *Milton's Grand Style,* (Oxford: The Clarendon Press, 1963)

Samuel, Irene. *Dante and Milton.* (Ithaca, N.Y.: Cornell University Press, 1966)

Sozzi, B. T. "La Poetica del Tasso." *Studi Tassiani* 5 (1955), repr. Bergamo: Centro Tassiano (1963): 7–70.

Spingarn, Joel E. *A History of Literary Criticism in the Renaissance.* New York: Macmillan, 1899; repr. New York: Harcourt, Brace and World, 1963.

Steadman, John M. *Epic and Tragic Structure in "Paradise Lost."* Chicago: University of Chicago Press, 1976.

———. *Milton and the Renaissance Hero.* Oxford: Clarendon Press, 1967.

Stein, Arnold. *Answerable Style.* Seattle: University of Washington Press, 1967.

Tillyard, E. M. W. *The English Epic and Its Background.* New York: Oxford University Press, 1966.

Weinberg, Bernard. *A History of Literary Criticism in the Italian Renaissance.* Chicago: University of Chicago Press, 1961.

Willey, Basil. *The Seventeenth Century Background.* 1934. Reprint ed., Garden City, N.Y.: Doubleday Anchor Books.

Williams, Arnold. *The Common Expositor: An Account of the Commentaries on Genesis, 1527–1633.* Chapel Hill: University of North Carolina Press, 1948.

Index